Hope y~
my cha~
entire

MASTER YOUR FINANCIAL SUCCESS

RETIREMENT AND LEGACY SECRETS FROM PLANNING PROFESSIONALS

AUTHORS PLACE
— P R E S S —

Published by Authors Place Press
9885 Wyecliff Drive, Suite 200
Highlands Ranch, CO 80126
Authorsplace.com

Financial planners featured in the book include: Briggs A. Matsko, Jeffrey R. Maas, Douglas E. Knable, Kelly L. Kennedy, Paula D. Tarpey, Paul A. Gydosh, Jr, Craig C. Bartlett, Philip G. Moshier, Michael McFeeley, Alex Harrison, J. Louis McCraw, Tyler R. McCraw, Derek B. Ferriera, J. Todd Anderson

Manufactured in the United States of America.

ISBN: 978-1-62865-671-8

CONTENTS

DISCLAIMER

The authors are registered representatives of Lincoln Financial Advisors Corp. Securities offered through Lincoln Financial Advisors Corp., a broker/dealer (member SIPC). Investment advisory services offered through Lincoln Financial Advisors or Sagemark Consulting, a division of Lincoln Financial Advisors Corp., a registered investment advisor. Insurance offered through Lincoln affiliates and other fine companies.

Marketing names used in the book are associated with the individual authors and are not an affiliate of Lincoln Financial Advisors.

Lincoln Financial Advisors Corp. and its representatives do not provide legal or tax advice. You may want to consult a legal or tax advisor regarding any legal or tax information as it relates to your personal circumstances.

The material here reflects the views of the author and not necessarily those of Lincoln Financial Advisors or its affiliates. This material is intended for educational purposes only and should not be used as investment advice or recommendations.

This book highlights important industry regulations and concepts. Please review these resources and concepts and consult your tax, financial, and legal professionals before implementing or making changes in a retirement plan.

Annuities are long-term retirement savings or income vehicles. There are fixed and variable annuities available; variable annuities are sold by prospectus. An investor should carefully consider the investment objectives, risks, charges, and expenses of the variable product and its underlying investment options carefully before investing. The prospectus contains this and other information about the variable product and its underlying investment options. Always read it carefully before investing.

INTRODUCTION

The authors of this book came together and unanimously agreed that we wanted to give back by educating others how to address several meaningful areas that impact everyone's financial planning lives. We are hopeful you will learn something new and be inspired to action at the same time, as even the best intentions that are never implemented can prove worthless, if not tragic.

Please use your newfound knowledge as power to plan for yourself and for those you care about most. It is through your personal improvement that our book becomes a success. We appreciate you reading it, and more importantly, we value the results you gain from it.

It was truly an honor and a journey for each of us to write this book alongside our peers. Without sounding too boastful, each of us is not only an extremely knowledgeable financial planning generalist but also an expert in the specific area in which we each wrote our chapter. It has been an opportunity for growth of our breadth of knowledge as we continuously absorb strategic advice from each other—an experience that propels us to improve the impact on and engagement with our clients.

To our clients, thank you for trusting us and allowing us to serve you all these years. Without you, this book would not have been possible.

To our staff, your unwavering dedication means the world to our clients as well as to us. For that we extend our sincere and genuine appreciation for all that you do.

To our families, thank you for your support not only through the process of writing *Master Your Financial Success*, but day in and day out as we built our careers. We have greatly appreciated your understanding during those long days and sleepless nights spent serving our clients.

And to our readers, go forth and strive to "Master Your Financial Success." We wish you the very best and wholeheartedly thank you for reading our book.

Please note that all authors of this book are registered representatives of Lincoln Financial Advisors Corp.

J. Todd Anderson	Jeffrey R. Maas
Craig C. Bartlett	Briggs A. Matsko
Derek B. Ferriera	J. Louis McCraw
Paul A. Gydosh, Jr	Tyler McCraw
Alex Harrison	Michael C. McFeeley
Kelly L. Kennedy	Philip Moshier
Douglas E. Knable	Paula Tarpey

DEDICATION

This book, and more specifically the chapter I authored on Generational Wealth Planning, is dedicated to my loving family, my devoted team at Wealth by Design and to our loyal clients. Your combined support, entrusting belief and unwavering commitment has permitted me to live my passion for financial planning which in return has provided purpose and meaning on so many levels to me, my family and our clients. For that and more, I extend my sincere, genuine and heart-felt "THANK YOU"!

ACKNOWLEDGEMENT

At this stage in my life, it is primarily my two daughters (Paige and Cora) who give me the strength, motivation and energy to accomplish anything and everything. You specifically have given my life purpose, meaning and personal fulfillment than one can ever express. I love you deeply and dearly.

My parents, Edna and Bill, have provided me a dream life, taught me so many valuable lessons and have always been my guiding light no matter how dark things can sometimes appear. Couple this with my 5 siblings and their spouses, and it is a never-ending sea of support, good times and laughter usually from some innocent and well deserved ribbing.

Craig C. Bartlett

CHAPTER ONE

RETIREMENT IS A NEW DAWN!

By Briggs A. Matsko & Jeffrey R. Maas

GET READY!

You are about to enter another dimension—your next journey in life! It will be a "New Dawn," and life is about to dramatically change. On this journey, you will become the master of your calendar, and each day will feel like Saturday. You will get to pursue your dreams and passions while creating new ones along the way. You will have a thousand epiphanies. You may wonder how you ever had time for work all those years . . .

Now it's time to **Define Your Future!** Are your thoughts already well defined, or are they abstract, or maybe a little of both? (Clue: there is no "right" answer.) Have you prioritized your dreams? Do you have a master plan? Remember, retirement is not black and white; it is a thousand shades of gray and will constantly change over the years (and that is okay).

It will also most certainly not be your parents' retirement! Our generation is living longer—seventy is the new fifty—and many of us will live well into our nineties! With medical advances coupled with healthier lifestyles, there is a 20-30 percent chance or better that we may live into our nineties (www.businessinsider.com/social-security-life-table-charts-2014-3).

This means you may find yourself in this New Dawn for twenty to thirty years. So, take some time to dream and plan the days, weeks, months, and years of your upcoming journey because retirement is not just an economic event—it is a life-planning event.

Over many decades of practice, we have found that many clients we meet with have very abstract ideas about retirement. They say, "I'm going to garden," or, "I'd like to play golf." We give them a blank calendar and say, "Fill it up with those activities," (which still leaves a lot of space) then ask, "Now what are you going to do the rest of the time?"

Like any journey, having a plan is always best, but it can be built on a flexible chassis (every minute does not have to be accounted for!). Consequently, we have created a Doctrine, which hangs on all our conference room walls, to inspire our clients to define their New Dawn.

©2011 Retirement Security Centers. All Rights Reserved.

We received so much positive feedback about this document that we created a video, which can be viewed on YouTube by searching for "RSC Doctrine" or on our website at www.defineyourfuture.com. All of the actors are clients and friends. We had a great time making it!

Perhaps you have heard of professionals who specialize in life coaching. Interestingly, there is a whole new brand of coaches who specialize in retirement life coaching. In fact, we have created affiliations with some of these coaches as a value-added benefit to our clients.

We find this to be particularly helpful to married couples that suddenly find themselves spending much more time together. After all, your spouse may not like you telling him or her how to load the dishwasher! Also, for many of you, your career has been your identity. Much of your life (and socialization) has been through your job or profession.

The sudden paradigm shift into a New Dawn can be disturbing. We have found that retirement coaching professionals can help people and couples think through some of the critical issues. In any event, spending some time planning your new journey and dreaming about your retirement is an important first step.

EASE INTO RETIREMENT

In our Doctrine, you may have noticed one of our sayings: Ease into Retirement. We believe that with proper planning the probability of success increases dramatically, not only from a life-planning standpoint, but financially as well. Consequently, we use the acronym **EASE** to describe our diagnostic process.

THE EASE PROCESS

Let us define these four important steps in more detail.

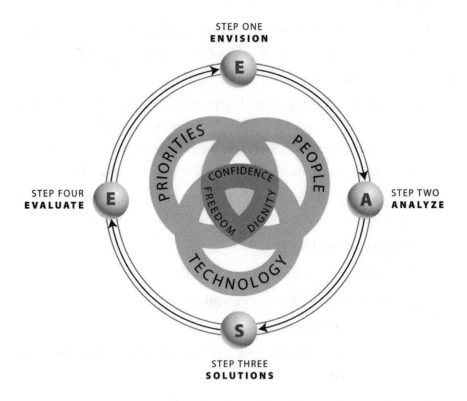

ENVISION

As we discussed, retirement is not just an economic event; it is a life-planning event. Most of us look forward to retirement and the perceived freedom that it brings.

The more you can define your dreams and activities (and the amount of time you will spend enjoying them), the greater the probability of your having a satisfying life in this new dimension. Sometimes it requires some negotiation with your spouse and/or children (or even yourself).

Creating your JOY mission is important. Have you created a bucket list? As you think about this New Dawn, questions arise, such as:

- **Where will you live?**
- **How often and where will you travel?**
- **What would you like to accomplish?**
- **What are your priorities?**
- **What are your expectations and how do they align with your family and friends?**
- **How will you continue to strive for optimal fulfillment?**

Remember, it is okay to change your mind, so don't get paralyzed by the thought that every decision is permanent. In fact, our experience with clients is that over the years their retirement ends up looking very different than what they initially imagined. It may be helpful to seek out the help of this new breed of retirement life coaches that are emerging on the scene. After you have "defined your future" with regard to lifestyle, dreams, and goals, it is time for your life planning to meet the economic events of retirement. At Retirement Security Centers we abide by the following philosophy:

"Our mission is to make sure that our clients do not outlive their money, especially for their core expenses, so they can maintain their financial independence, economic freedom, and dignity"

One of the primary questions we ask our clients is, "When you think of your retirement, have you thought about how to categorize your expenses and link them to your assets and income sources?" We have found that many of our clients have difficulty thinking about all the expenses they might have in retirement. In fact, studies show that up to 63 percent of Americans have difficulty categorizing and planning for expenses in retirement (www.Forbes.com, January 6, 2016).

Through our years of research and experience working with clients, we have developed a simple matrix, represented by our **pyramid**, which identifies many of the expenses you can expect in retirement.

We have categorized them into three primary areas: **CORE, JOY, and LEGACY**. Additionally, we have matched what we believe are the most appropriate potential income sources to fund these expenses.

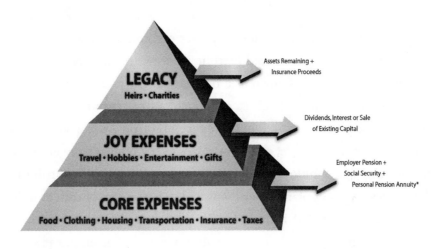

©2004, 2006, 2013 Retirement Security Centers. All Rights Reserved.

CORE EXPENSES

At the bottom, or foundation, of the pyramid, we have what we refer to as the CORE expenses we will have in retirement. We refer to them as

CORE because they are the ongoing, recurring expenses you will have as long as you live.

They are divided into six sub-categories: Food, Clothing, Housing, Transportation, Insurance, and Taxes. These are CORE because they are fundamental to maintaining your financial independence, security, and dignity in retirement.

Much of this can be defined by you; for example, one of our clients said his country club dues would be considered a CORE expense, not a JOY (non-essential) expense, so we put it in the CORE category.

Because these expenses are ongoing and recurring, we believe they should be satisfied with income sources that you will not outlive. As you can see, we have listed three sources of such income: (1) some Employer Pensions, (2) Social Security, and (3) what we refer to as "Personal Pension Annuities."

(1) The reason we say "some employer pensions" is that not all pension plans provide a guaranteed lifetime income stream. Specifically, we are referring to what is known as a defined benefit or cash balance plan that offers the options to receive a *guaranteed income from the plan for life*. Most of these plans are based on some type of formula that takes into account age, years of service, and your salary over time with the employer. In contrast, some employer plans are referred to as defined contribution plans. These types of plans typically provide a lump sum of cash at retirement, not a guaranteed income for life (they may be employer-funded only, or a combination of your contributions and your employer's contributions, plus accrued interest or gains). Some examples are 401(k)s, 403(b)s, 401(a) profit-sharing plans, Sep-IRAs, etc. We find that many of our clients are concerned about spending down or outliving this type of asset.

(2) Social Security benefits, as you may know, are a lifetime income stream that can be taken as early as age sixty-two. We typically create a Social Security Analysis for our clients to develop a strategy determining

how to best optimize benefits while meeting income needs. This may suggest taking benefits at age sixty-two, at Full Retirement Age, at age seventy, or anywhere in between, and would include additional strategies such as Spousal benefits.

(3) This brings me to the third income source—"Personal Pension Annuity." An annuity is typically a contract purchased from an insurance company that will guarantee a *lifetime income stream* in exchange for a cash payment, or premium. These guarantees are backed by the claims-paying ability of the issuer of the contract. There are many different types of payout options to choose from, and you can customize plans to meet your personal needs, hence the term "Personal Pension Annuity."

JOY EXPENSES

The next level is what we refer to as JOY expenses. These typically are the "fun" things we would like to do in retirement, but not essential to our well-being. Because people have such a wide variety of interests, it is impossible to list them all.

Instead, we have identified some of the most common categories: Travel, Hobbies, Entertainment, and Gifts. However, you can include any other goals and bucket-list items you might be thinking about.

While there are many ways to pay for these expenses (including guaranteed income sources from the previous category), we believe that one of the most prudent ways to fund JOY expenses is from dividends and interest on existing assets.

This enables you to gauge or budget the amount you might want to spend on this category without depleting your principal. You may also want to use some income sources from your CORE category to help fund part, or all, of these expenses. You may even consider selling existing assets, such as a coin collection or a boat, to fund some of these expenses.

LEGACY EXPENSES

Finally, we have reached the top of the pyramid, which we refer to as the LEGACY level. This refers to those assets that you might want to pass through to your heirs or charities after your death.

Typically, this consists of whatever financial holdings you have not spent, property, and insurance proceeds. While most people are concerned primarily about the first two categories of CORE and JOY expenses, it is important to consider what your wishes might be with regard to your LEGACY.

First and foremost, you should have a will, trust, or some other legal document to deal with the distribution of your remaining assets at death. Assets from all three of the prior categories may flow through your estate, and it is important to understand your options. Proper planning will help you maximize the wealth you transfer, minimize the impact of taxes, and keep the state you live in from deciding it for you!

ANALYZE

The next step in the **EASE** process after you have categorized your assets, income sources, and expenses is to analyze how they impact the four major risks in retirement, which we define as follows:

1. LONGEVITY: As we said previously, many of you will live well into your nineties, which means you could spend twenty to thirty years watching expenses increase with inflation while you are drawing down assets and managing income sources. The question is how much is enough? Will you outlive your assets? What is your current health situation, and how have you insured against future health issues beyond Medicare coverage (for instance, long term care events, which are mostly not covered by Medicare or standard medical insurance plans)?

2. EXPENSES: What is your budget (for both CORE and JOY expenses) in retirement, and are you adjusting it for the various stages in retired life, which we refer to as the early (Go-Go years), the mid (Slow-Go years), and the late (No-Go years)? Most web-based computer models use linear assumptions and do not take into consideration these adjustments, so they tend to project inaccurately.

3. RATE OF RETURN: Do you currently have an investment policy statement to determine what rate of return you need to get on your investments so as not to run out of money? If so, what science or formula did you use to arrive at this number? The portfolio mix you used in the accumulation phase (accumulating assets while working) may not be the same portfolio mix you should use when you are using income sources to cover expenses in retirement. How do you maximize yield while mitigating risk? How do you determine a rate of return that will insure you do not prematurely draw down your assets?

4. INFLATION: This is the foundation of any projection in a long-term financial plan and one over which we have no control, but must constantly measure. While inflation over the last decade has been relatively low, a return to the high inflation of the seventies and eighties can be a disaster to those who are retired and living on a fixed income. Take a look at newspaper ads from twenty to thirty years ago and see what things cost then. Think about the price of a postage stamp, a gallon of gasoline, or a loaf of bread back in those days. A 1 percent assumption as the average rate of inflation on a linear basis over twenty to thirty years can make a significant difference in the probability of financial success in retirement.

Trying to solve for any one of these risks alone, much less simultaneously, is a daunting task. Consequently, achieving a proper diagnosis and strategy requires sophisticated software to determine the probable outcome to create different "what-if" scenarios.

While there are various tools/calculators on the Web suited to this purpose, we have found that most are limited in their functions and do not take into consideration the vast number of variables that need to be considered to create more accurate results.

Our firm, after years of development and refinement, has developed a software program that accounts for most variables and allows us to illustrate quickly and succinctly multiple scenarios using a wide variety of assumptions. By illustrating these various "what-ifs" with graphics and images versus reams of spreadsheets, we are able to easily convey complex projections in a clear and concise manner.

We do this interactively on a large monitor and work in collaboration with our clients to arrive at the best plan going forward. Our advice is to find a professional CERTIFIED FINANCIAL PLANNER™ who is skilled in the use of similar interactive software to assist you in this effort.

©2011 Retirement Security Centers. All Rights Reserved.

SOLUTIONS

Once the diagnostic analysis has been performed, we generally find that there is either not enough money (a shortfall) to last over a retirement lifetime or there is more than enough, which means that there are other things to consider that are more positive.

Let us begin with the shortfall scenario. To solve for this we use a process we call SOS, which everyone knows is the acronym for help or distress. However our SOS stands for the "Seven Optional Solutions" that can be implemented to correct shortfalls and increase the probabilities of success. They are as follows:

1. WORK LONGER: Every year you continue to work gives an average of two to three years of financial security in retirement (based on our software modeling). The reasoning is that you not only would be earning money for expenses—and hopefully continuing to save for the long term—but you would not be spending the money you have saved; thus, savings would continue to earn interest and grow.

2. ADJUST LIFE EXPECTANCY or DIE SOONER: This is a bit of a "tongue-in-cheek" option that gets a laugh from most of our clients. Obviously, most of us want to live as long as possible with good health. The fact is most of us will have longer lives than our parents. However, if genetically (we are learning more and more about this lately) we are predisposed to certain illnesses, such as heart disease, or our parents or other family members die at a relatively young age, then this may be a consideration. However, for the most part we plan for longevity to age ninety-five.

3. SPEND LESS: When clients estimate budgets in retirement, we tell them to dream unabated at first, especially for the JOY expenses. This gives us the opportunity to help them prioritize if they have to cut back. We also focus on the CORE expenses and discuss downsizing their house, for instance, or take into consideration not having to buy work clothes or pay for things like dry cleaning. Proper tax

planning and liquidation order also fall into this category. The less we owe in taxes in retirement through proper planning, the more we can allocate to other expenditures.

4. SAVE MORE: If clients still have another five to ten years or longer before retirement (we call this being in the "Sprint"), then we encourage them to set aside a bigger portion toward long-term savings and to be sure to maximize any tax-deferred (401(k), 403(b), IRA) or tax-free savings (Roth, Muni Bonds) before retirement.

5. INCREASE RATE OF RETURN: Since we manage most of our clients' investments, many of them favor this option since it switches the responsibility from them to us. However, we are quick to point out that while we can target whatever rate of return they want, the risk factor goes up the more we endeavor to increase the return, and the volatility also increases (especially if investing in equities). We do not like to assume (given today's economic environment of nearly 0 percent in fixed income rates) more than 6 percent as a long-term annualized return in retirement. The average comfort level is a 4 percent return. The reasoning is that the more stock market exposure we have, the more we are subject to the volatility of the markets. Obviously, volatility is not ideal when one is withdrawing principal and gains to meet living expenses. The investment policy statement is predicated upon an agreed projected rate of return and an annual (or more frequent) reevaluation. This is critical to achieving a high probability of financial success in retirement.

6. ADJUST INFLATION ASSUMPTIONS: Like the rate of return, this is also a tempting way to reduce projected deficits in retirement. It is surprising what a 1 percent difference in inflation can do (either good or bad) over a thirty-year distribution plan. Hence, it is critical not to assume too low of a rate. We like to use a 3.5 percent inflation rate since that is the long-term average over the last thirty years, even though the current average is lower. It

is important to illustrate the differences inflation can make over long periods of time so that clients don't find themselves surprised by it years after they have retired and perhaps can no longer find desirable employment or even re-engage in the workforce.

7. COMBINATION: In reality, it usually is not just one of the previous Solutions that will "fix" the situation. While one solution may have a greater effect, like working longer, it is generally applying a combination of all of the different solutions that achieves a high probability of success for the client. We illustrate this interactively with our software on a "what-if basis," which shows our clients a variety of different scenarios and lets them pick the one that is most desirable and realistic based on current data in conjunction with various assumptions.

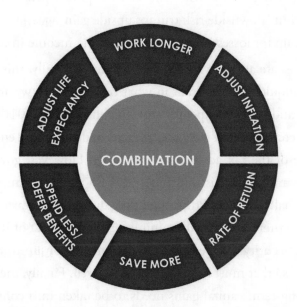

SOS The Seven Optional Solutions

In addition to the SOS shortfall solutions above, experienced financial planners will also take into considerations the following:

Rebalancing. We find that portfolio rebalancing is a primary consideration. There is usually a significant difference in philosophy between the accumulation phase and the retirement phase. During the income distribution phase in retirement we are usually more concerned about the loss of principal than we are about maximizing yield. In fact, when we pointed this out to our client, Jerry, he asked, "Are you telling me to reduce my market exposure?" What Jerry didn't realize was that he had finally saved enough, and given his projected needs he did not have to take the risks inherent in the stock market. He only needed a 3 percent rate of return, so we told him that we were solving for "the need, not the greed." We certainly could have maintained a high degree of market exposure, but why take the risk? This can be quite a paradigm shift for most people, but "downside risk trumps upside gain" when we don't have time to make up for losses and we are not earning income in retirement.

Taxes. Taxes are always a big consideration. Generally, this involves a discussion of liquidation order, as in what types of assets we are going to draw on first and last. Most people have qualified assets (401(k), 403(b), 401(a), IRA, etc.) that they have contributed to during their employment years because of the tax advantages they offer. However, governmental rules require minimum distributions of these assets beginning at age seventy and a half (RMDs). Proper planning during lower taxable income years in early retirement can help minimize the tax impact of RMDs later in life. Social Security can be subject to income tax on up to 85 percent of the benefit, so that must be kept in mind as well. Finally, the impact of short- and long-term capital gains needs to be taken into consideration, along with other special tax exemptions on the sale of primary residential real estate.

Gifting. Gifting strategies can be very important for those clients who have more than enough and want to pass on assets to heirs or charity.

Much of this is discussed in other chapters and includes many of the trusts and foundations that can be established to create favorable tax treatment and maximize the transfer of wealth both before and after death.

Risk Management. One of the most important components to consider is what we call "risk management strategies." In other words, are you adequately insured in retirement? Our client, Mitch, said to us recently, "Now that my family is grown and we have so much in assets, I am going to cash out and drop my life insurance policies." While this might seem like a sound strategy on the surface, Mitch did not think about the fact that he chose to receive his defined benefit pension as a "single life" option to be paid during his lifetime only, not to his spouse, Joanna, in the event of his death. This means that if Mitch were to predecease Joanna, she would no longer have that paycheck. In addition, her Social Security benefit would change to the highest amount between them, but only one check would be received. After taking all this into consideration, Mitch decided to keep some of the life insurance to make up for those lost income streams. In addition, life insurance can be an effective way to pay for estate taxes for those above the personal unified exemption credit. Life insurance can also create an immediate defined estate for heirs or charity so that spending down inheritable assets is less of a concern for those clients wishing to leave a legacy.

Another risk-management strategy is long-term care. With longer life spans, the probability of needing long-term care increases. In fact, according to the US Department of Health and Human Services (*HHS. gov*), one in two sixty-five plus year olds will need long-term care services. We see many people confuse Medicare and acute care coverage with long-term care coverage. Understanding the differences is extremely important. Many people think that this won't be a problem for them; however, the odds suggest differently, and when we model it as a "what-if" scenario, the results cause our clients to think more about why they should consider some type of long-term care coverage versus self-insuring.

Buckets. We also believe in the so-called "bucket strategies," which basically segregate assets into short- (one to three years), intermediate (three to seven years), and long-term (seven years and beyond) buckets. The short-term assets are placed in typically low yield, highly liquid assets (money markets, savings accounts, cash or ultra-short floating rate accounts) to allow for liquidity regardless of market performance or other variables. The intermediate assets are placed in a more moderate portfolio (some bond funds, value dividend paying stocks, etc.) so they can grow and eventually replenish the short-term bucket. Finally, the long-term bucket (growth stocks, longer-term bonds and alternative investments such as REITS, commodities, etc.) is positioned to allow for more growth over the long run and to eventually replenish the intermediate bucket. This is a good way for clients to understand their portfolio construction and liquidation order in retirement.

Creating actionable goals and implementing them is the key to successful solutions in retirement distribution planning. It is important to remember that no "one size fits all" or "rule of thumb" strategy should be the foundation of the plan. Since retirement can be a thousand shades of gray, it is important to build your most realistic, customized scenario based on your personal situation. This is why it is important for most people to work with a financial professional who can diagnose and then create a customized solution, a plan that can be measured, monitored, and implemented; a plan for a sense of financial security.

EVALUATE

Measure, measure, measure! "What gets measured gets done." Briggs was taught this by his mentor, Nick Horn.

We believe that distribution planning for retirement is not just a one-time event; it is an ongoing process.

We share this philosophy with all our clients, and it is the reason why EVALUATE is the fourth, and maybe the most important, step in our **EASE** process.

We explain to our clients that any projection we make for a long period such as twenty to thirty years is eventually going to veer off course. This leads to some interesting reactions, especially after a lot of collaboration to come up with a realistic plan. The reason, we tell them, is that "life gets in the way."

Children move back home or need a loan. Someone may get sick and need care. Investments do not perform exactly to projections. Inflation goes up. Governmental policies and regulations change. Someone gets a large inheritance or wins the lottery. You name it, but life gets in the way.

This is why we do, at minimum, an annual checkup or report card. We ask clients to fill out their datasheet again. Have their expenses been higher or lower than expected? If higher, was it a one-time expenditure, like a home remodel, or will it be an ongoing expense, like higher utility or medical bills?

How did the portfolio perform? Was it on target, better, or worse than the investment policy statement? Were there any life-changing events or things outside their control, like inflation, illness, family emergencies, or natural disasters? All of these things influence the plan going forward and must be accounted for.

The plan needs to be refined, assumptions adjusted, solutions scrutinized, portfolios checked, and risk management reassessed. Most of the time only small adjustments are needed, but over the long run these make a big difference. It is much better for clients to reevaluate than wait five years and find out they are running out of money.

The first few years in retirement are especially crucial, as most people do not really know what to expect. They haven't been down this path before. It is the difference between conjecture and reality. We also joke that people change from Dr. Jekyll to Mr. Hyde when it comes to watching their money.

All of the sudden their savings are being drained, and no matter how much they have planned, it can be alarming. They wonder if the money is really going to last. "I did not expect this expense or anticipate that new hobby," they say. All of these things must be taken into consideration and planned for by consistent evaluation, refining, and revision of the plan.

It is also important to plan for the various stages in retirement, from both an economic- and a life-planning perspective. After working with hundreds of people in retirement, we have found the early, mid, and late stages of retirement look very different.

As mentioned earlier, we have named them "Go-Go," "Slow-Go," and "No-Go." Go-Go is generally the first ten to fifteen years of retirement when you are healthy and still have the energy to travel, garden, golf, or whatever your JOY desires may be.

Slow-Go is generally the next five to ten years, where the travel is less and may be done closer to home; physical activities and hobbies get scaled back or become less frequent. Finally, No-Go is when we start to cocoon. We spend more time at home; the children come to visit us instead of us going to see them. Maybe our health doesn't permit us to do as much.

It is a time for reflection, gratitude, and perhaps to focus more on our spirituality. We admit this does not apply to everyone, but after working with people in retirement for over forty years, it is generally the norm. How would you define your three phases in retirement?

SUMMARY AND FINAL THOUGHTS

Briggs's mentor, Nick Horn, often told him, "Honest, intelligent effort is always rewarded." If you take the time to plan for your retirement for both the life planning as well as the economic event, you will be more successful than most people. If you review and refine your plan at least once a year you will be even more successful.

Do you want to do it yourself, or do you want professional help customized to your situation? If so, take the time to choose the right professional. They should be willing to use a diagnostic, process-driven approach and not be interested in only selling you a product.

We would suggest that when it comes time to make the most important financial decisions of your lifetime, you consider a credentialed advisor. A credentialed planner has taken the time to get additional education, pass a rigorous exam, is required to do continued education, and abides by ethical standards to maintain their designations.

Make sure there is transparency and you have an understanding about what you are paying for along with fees and/or commissions.

With over fifty-five years of collective experience as financial planners, our experience is that those clients who have properly planned for their golden years have found retirement to be extremely rewarding. Remember, retirement planning is not just a one-time event, but an ongoing process.

Define your future, have fun, and enjoy your **NEW DAWN!**

Professional Profile:

Briggs A. Matsko, CFP°, CRPC°

Briggs.Matsko@RSCenters.com | 916-868-3900 |

www.DefineYourFuture.com

Briggs Matsko is a financial planner and co-founder of Retirement Security Centers. His firm specializes in diagnosing and providing solutions for the income distribution needs of those approaching or already in retirement. Briggs believes this planning is an ongoing process, not a one-time event.

Briggs began his financial planning career over forty years ago when he joined Lincoln Financial Advisors, and since that time he has built his reputation as a client advocate. His objective, process-driven approach to financial guidance takes into consideration not only quantitative data but his vast experience in understanding clients' needs, goals, and desires.

Briggs obtained his CERTIFIED FINANCIAL PLANNER™ practitioner certification in 1994 and earned his CHARTERED RETIREMENT PLANNING COUNSELOR™ designation in 2010.

Briggs is a thought leader and is regularly sought out to share his knowledge and perspectives in the financial services industry. He has been featured in various publications, such as *Research Magazine* and *Boomer Market Advisor*. His speaking engagements include Million Dollar Round Table's annual meetings, the Retirement Income Industry Association, NAVA, and various other national industry venues.

Briggs, his wife, Cynthia, and their son, Reed, live in Northern California. He enjoys golf and fishing as well as being actively involved in his community.

Professional Profile:
Jeffrey R. Maas, CFP°, ChFC°, CRPC°

Jeff.Maas@RSCenters.com | 916-868-3900 |

www.DefineYourFuture.com

Jeffrey Maas, a co-founder and Financial Planner affiliated with Retirement Security Centers, specializes in meeting the financial planning needs of those approaching or having already entered retirement.

Jeff began his financial planning career in 2003. His passion and expertise in retirement planning is coupled with his ongoing extensive demographic and economic research, which drives the lives of millions of aging Americans. His track record with hundreds of retirees has him regularly called upon for commentary, speaking engagements, and television appearances with national media, industry associations, and his peers.

As a CERTIFIED FINANCIAL PLANNER™ practitioner, Jeff delivers an objective and process-based approach that takes into consideration not only clients' economics but also their values and ambitions. It is his mission to help clients achieve a crystallized vision of their retirement from a psychological and financial perspective so they can proudly live with a sense of security in those decisions.

Jeff graduated with a bachelor's degree in Business Administration with a double major in Finance and Management from California State University, Chico. He served on the Board of Directors for the Financial Planning Association of Northern California.

Jeff and his family currently reside in Rancho Murieta, California.

CHAPTER TWO

FINANCIAL STEWARDSHIP

By Douglas E. Knable & Kelly L. Kennedy

WHAT IS FINANCIAL STEWARDSHIP?

While we all have different goals and objectives in life, in this chapter we will view financial stewardship as the positive utilization and continual improvement of your God-given Time, Talents, and Treasury. We all come into life with nothing and leave life with nothing, but what we do in-between with those gifts speaks volumes in our ability to be a good steward. We all are given a variable amount of time as well as different amounts and types of talents and treasury, but it is our growth and utilization of each that will define our worthiness as a credible steward.

Thinking of the ways to progress through life, in this chapter we will focus and reflect on improved utilization of the time, talent, and treasury that remain for each of us. Regardless of the time that remains, current level of our talent, or the amount of treasury we have to work with, improved stewardship always exists.

Proper financial stewardship exponentially increases value; conversely, improper financial stewardship dramatically dilutes value. Many have heard the saying, "Cost is only an issue in the absence of value." I often add the follow-up: "Lack of value is a cost few of us can bear."

STORY TIME: A TALE OF TWO FATHERS

I was blessed with two wonderful fathers during my life, my father and my father-in-law. They both showed great degrees of financial stewardship. One spent his career working at a large corporation for others. He knew that was not the destiny that was meant for his life, nor the summation of his life's work for others to recall. So with the help of a savvy financial advisor he was able to retire at age fifty, to enjoy a full, active retirement that lasted longer than his work career, supplanting his efforts serving others in retirement as his life's legacy.

Conversely, my other father showed great stewardship in that he was the longtime head of a family business that had been in existence for well over a hundred years. He saw it as a great calling and challenge in life to be a good business steward, assuring that he could pass the baton to future generations just as his ancestors had provided him the opportunity to thrive and continue serving so many clients, employees, and his community.

Where one retired early to fulfill his life's legacy, another chose to stay with the family business for over sixty years until he was finally able to pass the torch to future generations. The key would be that they both retained the passion for their work until a new passion came along. While one individual may choose to work for his money only until his money is able to provide a quality income for his family, for others, an early life passion may last a lifetime.

KEYS TO SUCCESS

The keys to success and positive financial stewardship in life often include many of the following:

- **The Golden Rule—Do Unto Others as You Would Have Them Do unto You.** A version of this rule has been a part of almost every religion since the beginning of recorded time. This succinct statement has served endless generations well. Always think of others first, put yourself in their position, and assist them in choosing their best course of action.

- **Have a Plan.** Ben Franklin summed it up well, "Failing to plan is planning to fail." A must for financial stewardship is having a plan, executing that plan, and constantly reviewing, grading, and improving your plan. The endless circle of Plan, Execute, and Review is essential in small, medium, and large endeavors. Whether planning for a small dinner party, annual growth in your business, or coordinating your life, always have a plan and execute your plan with vigor. By all means, constantly review and improve your plan. Plan, Execute and Review—those are three key underpinnings of financial stewardship.

- **Be Prepared.** For over one hundred years the timeless Scout motto, "Be Prepared," has blazed the trail for many a good steward. Being prepared includes being knowledgeable, educated, motivated, and action-oriented to consummate the desired outcome. Whether the task is completed yourself or by another, you remain prepared to see the issue through to the best of your ability.

- **Live Within Your Means.** It is amazing how often in life the simplest or basic keys to success are not followed. However, any individual who consistently lives within their means is a wealthy individual and well on their way to proper financial stewardship. How do you live within your means? No matter how much you make, spend less. If you do not think you make enough to set aside a portion, create a plan for enhanced income or begin reducing your financial commitments and lifestyle. Either way, a good financial steward consistently lives within their means.

Living within your means includes paying yourself first. Every month there will always be a list of bills for us to pay. Whether your stack of bills includes a utility or phone bill, taxes, insurance, etc., every month should also include a payment to improve your future.

If you do not take the time to plan for your own future and pay yourself first, you have little chance of ever being in the position to have your money working for you. Ultimately, by living within your means you will achieve a point in life where, instead of working for money, your money can work for you, assuring your future financial lifestyle can be maintained. The commitment to these very basic principles, "Live within your means and pay yourself first," are vital steps toward quality financial stewardship.

The Rule of 75/25 is another that has stood the test of time. The objective of 75/25 is to set aside 25 percent of your income, regardless of the amount, for savings, accumulation, and your future while committing to live on only the remaining 75 percent. By committing to this plan you will always have an increasing pool of funds focused on increasing the accumulation in your retirement accounts, education accounts, and other personal investments, enhancing the possibility of attaining your overall life goals and objectives. Keep in mind that less change in life often leads to more change in your pocket. While change can be advantageous, the cost of change is often understated. Remaining focused and committed to one's core beliefs in life often leads to a more stable and fulfilling life journey.

- **Always Act as a First-Generation Wealth Builder**. Many believe that once a family is wealthy their heirs will enjoy a wealthy lifestyle forever. That is not the case. During my career, I have seen, time and time again, cases involving previously wealthy families from which the first generation "grew" assets and lifestyles from rags to riches, only to be followed by the second generation who "managed" the family assets, which was then followed by the third generation who often focused on the "consumption" of wealth.

  What we have found is that whether you are in the first generation, the second generation, or third generation, as you make decisions in life, if you desire to be a good steward of wealth, do not act as a manager, do not act as a consumer, but act as a first-generation wealth builder. A healthy steward at all times keeps an eye on risk-adjusted growth, as this is the fuel that funds the building of wealth and financial stewardship.

- **Think Creatively, Take Educated Risks, and Grow.** Always be looking to grow; if you are not growing you are usually on the road to consumption. Focus on quality growth, eliminating unnecessary risks, and moving forward at all times.

STORY TIME: EVER THE FIRST-GENERATION, GROWTH-ORIENTED, RISK-TAKING BUSINESS OWNER

Another client of mine had a brilliant legal practice spanning over six decades. Finally retired in his early seventies, his wife thought that, as a quality servant to many generations of clients, he was finally ready to sit back and relax. A decade later, at age eighty, he received a call that changed his life. A glass factory that had been in his distant family was in disrepair. It had passed through a number of generations, and the current owners were no longer interested in the business, employees, or community, merely desiring to enjoy the historical business cash flow. Finding themselves on the verge of bankruptcy, the fifth-generation owners called my client at age eighty and asked him what they should do.

After much soul searching, my client came to the conclusion that none of the current owners wanted to work, so this eighty-year-old retiree concluded that what the business needed most was a new, first-generation-thinking entrepreneur. My client then bought them out and dove headfirst into returning this 170-year-old family business back to glory. For the next decade he remained dedicated to running it as a first-generation owner.

The results were astonishing. He had brought the family business back to its pristine place as a great community contributor and great employer. This individual provided all a clear example of how planning, preparedness, and thinking like a financial steward can bring quality results to all who step up, participating with vigor and wisdom.

THE VALUE OF EDUCATION

Accumulators and quality stewards embody the concept of lifelong learning. Whether in high school, when individuals are sure to study and prepare for their future, or in college, when students begin to "lean in" as they increase their preparedness for the future, or those that continue classroom education in the form of graduate degrees, financial stewards are constantly preparing for an improved future.

A lifelong commitment to furthering one's education is something that most individuals focused on financial stewardship find to be an essential and valuable asset. The value of an education is something that consistently comes back many times over, providing improvement and a return on investment for the individual, their family, and community.

Whether education occurs in the classroom or not, we recommend clients always keep an ear open to furthering their education.

STORY TIME: EVEN ON GRADUATION DAY, LEARNING CAN OCCUR

On graduation day, feeling full of knowledge, I floated across campus in my cap and gown. Little did I know I was about to have a profound educational moment. Feeling quite confident and pleased with myself, walking across campus I happened upon the Chair of the Economics department and thought I'd take a moment to share with him a bit of my promising future. With a confident wave, I said, "Professor, I thought you might be interested to hear what I will be doing after graduation?" He grumped but allowed me to continue.

I said, "Well, let me tell you, I already have five offers," and with much delight I went through each of them at length. The first four offered tremendous income, much more than anticipated. I barely mentioned the fifth one as it was an embarrassment because I felt the offer was so low. He listened quietly as we continued at his brisk walking pace, and then I asked, "Which of these should I choose?"

With a quick wave of his hand he immediately responded in a deep German accent, "Aughhhhh, you ask me such an elementary question. Have I not taught you anything? The first four you mention, they choose to pay you much more than you are worth. You have proven very little to them, your knowledge in their industry is at the absolute basic level, you are still worth very little to them. They are funding future hires at the expense of their seasoned valued employees; this means they must underpay you later in life when you have much to offer.

"However, the fifth company, they offer you what you are truly and currently worth to them, very little. This last company is willing to provide you an income commensurate with your true value, which I currently surmise is very little." A long, quiet pause occurred, then he smiled and concluded, "I recommend you sign with them! For if you are as good as I think you are, this career will pay you handsomely in the years to come. As they will always pay you what you are truly worth." And with that he was gone and my career path decision was forever altered.

Takeaways:

- Always be open for an opportunity to increase your education; you never know when it is coming.

- Value delivered, not time expended, is a better determinant for remuneration.

DIVERSIFICATION

While acting as a financial steward, proper diversification is essential. Let us start with asset classification. The three main investment classification areas include cash, bonds, and equities. Cash is primarily comprised of checking, savings, money markets, and short-term government obligations; these typically have very low yields but provide a low risk to principal and liquidity.

The second area includes bonds or debt instruments. Typically this would include lending to corporations of all sizes, both domestic and international, government, or municipal debt obligation issues. Simply stated, the lower the risk of failure or default potential of the loan, the lower the yield you should anticipate. Conversely, if you lend money to corporations of a higher default risk, a higher interest rate or premium should be anticipated.

US Government obligations are usually considered a low-risk investment; therefore their interest rate is typically on the smaller historical yield than other securities. Municipal authorities have an advantage of offering yields that include the income being tax free from various taxing authorities.

Equities carry more risk but offer greater reward potential in terms of appreciation and the protection of your purchasing power.

Duration: Investments should be made on both a short-term and long-term basis, complementing intelligent risk taking in the area of equities.

Liquidity: Money has little value if not available when needed. The liquidity of funds should always be accounted for as unanticipated needs will occur throughout life. To provide for this exposure, it is recommended that an appropriate amount of funds be deposited in short-term, liquid, low-risk positions such as cash, money markets, and short-term obligations.

Intelligent Risk Taking: This goes hand in hand with good stewardship of a portfolio. Historically speaking, quality equities are the primary avenue to maintaining purchasing power through the decades. Protecting one's purchasing power is of utmost importance.

The main obstacles causing erosion of an individual's purchasing power are taxation, inflation, and faulty risk analysis. One must remain vigilant of these adversaries on the journey of protecting purchasing power and financial stewardship.

Qualified and Non-Qualified Investments: Qualified investments typically include Traditional, Roth and Simple IRAs, SEPs, pension plans, 401(k)s, 403(b)s, etc. All have the tax advantage of deferred growth, and a few, such as Roth IRAs and 529s, have the added feature of potentially growing income tax free.

Those are valuable attributes, but they do not come without significant restrictions. Additionally, it is rarely advisable to borrow from your retirement plan. If possible, find another way to care for a current need. To protect against this occurrence it is strongly advised that as a financial steward you also create and invest in a non-qualified investment portfolio.

Takeaways:

- Every investment is a blend of advantage and disadvantage.

- There are very few times in life where you can expect great returns without taking a commensurate degree of risk.

- It is rarely about *timing* the market; it is normally about time *in* the market. Those who try to move money in and out in order to miss short-term negative repercussions in the market invariably miss the upside as well.

CONSUMERS AND ACCUMULATORS

Financially speaking, there are basically two groups of individuals. The first group possesses consumer tendencies, while the second is comprised of those who possess accumulator tendencies. The way to determine which camp an individual falls in would be to "follow the money." Do their excess funds tend to appreciate, or are they used to enhance additional consumption?

If their excess funds tend to be deployed in ways that appreciate, they are showing accumulator tendencies. On the other hand, if they often acquire assets that tend to go down in value, that would insinuate a typically consumer-oriented tendency.

The Burden of Consumer Debt: Consumer debt is a shackle on many individuals that precludes their ability to accumulate. Deferring full payment on consumer debt will ultimately drive up the total cost. Compounding the poor choice to defer full payment is that this added cost occurs as the value of that asset is declining. This creates a never-ending spiral that is rarely a part of successful financial stewardship.

Layaway programs often provided on furniture or other consumer items that you do not pay off on your credit card within thirty days are a significant drain on your financial future. Therefore, the only consumer debt that a good steward incurs is debt that you pay off immediately, thereby eliminating onerous interest charges, fees, and additional costs.

The Value of Potential Growth: While consumer debt is something to be eliminated from a financial steward perspective, potential growth can be advantageous. So far in this century, we have enjoyed very low interest rates. Low interest rates and loans at a low interest can allow you to control larger equity assets that have historically created much value.

Land, buildings, and business acquisitions; if acquired at a nominal interest rate and the asset appreciates, your rate of return is exponential due to the fact that you have only invested a portion of your capital, deploying the balance elsewhere while enjoying the appreciation potential of a larger asset base.

For example: Purchasing property for $500,000 in cash versus a down payment of $100,000 and borrowing the remaining $400,000. In the latter example, if all goes well and the property grows at a rate greater than the loan rate, the investor should enjoy exponential growth compared to the all-cash purchase.

Advanced use of leveraged growth can also occur via the borrowing power within an equity-based brokerage account that includes additional borrowing power limits. However, this concept should only be implemented by very astute investors in concert with their financial advisor team, as negative news can quickly result in margin calls, which could generate onerous negative returns.

Consumer Tendencies: Consumer tendencies include areas such as short-term debt, lifestyles in excess of income, expensive tastes in purchases of homes, cars, clubs, jewelry, etc. Acquisitions that do not create value consume value. Additional examples often include, but are not limited to, tickets for sporting events and the theatre. Not to suggest that we should never attend such enjoyable events, but one should always remember that this consumptive practice is a part of the 75 percent of their income and not to be taken from the 25 percent focused on accumulation.

Additional consumer tendencies include:

- Making purchases via layaway programs or infomercials that almost always begin to lose value from the very first day acquired.

- Lack of significant investment toward retirement or family education.

- The tendency to have an ever-increasing amount of debt.

- Any amount of consumer debt that is not paid off within the first thirty days. If not paid off quickly, you are exhibiting consumer tendencies, which are directly opposed to being a good financial steward. Consumer debt can be a drug that poisons your future.

If you exhibit many of these consumer tendencies, then your ability to be a good financial steward is currently being compromised. It would be advisable to include a professionally accredited financial advisor in your future financial decision process.

STORY TIME: THE RISING STAR WITH A CEO LIFESTYLE

Many years ago I began working with many senior executives of one of America's well-known corporations. Invariably, when thinking of others that I should meet, these senior executives all mentioned one rising star, on the fast track, as a key younger executive that I should meet. When I finally did meet with this individual, it was clear he had all the trappings of success.

He had a beautiful office, a gorgeous home, and all the toys any kid would want. His family was enjoying a backyard swimming pool, membership in the most expensive country club in town, luxury cars, and he wore the finest suits of any executive of that Fortune 500 company.

But when we sat down to talk about caring for his family and financial house, it was apparent that he did not have any savings for the education for his children, nor money set aside in his 401(k); he did not appear to have any assets that were appreciating. Instead of an investment account he had six credit cards that were maxed out and a highly leveraged home with an additional line of credit outstanding.

This individual was making more than almost anybody in his age bracket, yet it was not enough. He was spending at a rate way above his wage. He was making purchases his wages could not cover. Unfortunately I was unable to gain his ear, and then, very sadly, his wife became very ill. He then needed to hire someone to care for his children and wife while he continued to work, because he could not afford to take time off.

Having never accumulated anything, he had to begin terminating many of his memberships and obligations, starting with his country club, expensive cars, and care of his home. As you may suspect, his work began to suffer, and unfortunately he did not continue to be a rising star at that company.

We need to be prepared for life's margin calls. A good steward should always have an emergency fund built up, with a focus on accumulation and a desire to be a first-generation wealth builder. Those that focus on the consumption of wealth rarely remain accumulators and stewards of wealth.

ACCUMULATOR TENDENCIES

Accumulators tend to be contrarians to each of the previous points. They stay focused on the accumulation of real and appreciating assets. Stewards and acquirers of wealth have stood the test of time by focusing on the acquisition of assets that are maintaining or increasing purchasing power. Assets that historically increase purchasing power include: blue-chip equities, land, buildings, and family businesses. Accumulators also tend to focus on assets that provide annually increased income, allowing them to be greater stewards of wealth.

Do you tend to acquire assets that typically offer future income, growth, or increased dividend potential? Did your acquisitions in the last year have the opportunity to increase in value? Did you allocate 25 percent of your income in the past year to be set aside into assets that historically have grown in value?

STORY TIME: THE OFFICE SECRETARY

Another individual that I had the pleasure of working with for much of my career is a retired senior-level secretary from a local bank. She had worked at the bank most of her life but said she never owned a CD. When I first sat down with her she said, "I am not sure what I should be doing, but I think I really should speak with somebody who knows finance, and your name keeps popping up in our key client retention meetings."

She went on to talk about the things that she wanted to do in her life—helping her extended family and community involvement. Before she showed me her portfolio, I was thinking, "I am not sure how I can help her, because she does not appear to have had the opportunity to accumulate much."

How wrong I was! It turns out that she had lived on less than 75 percent of her income for much of her career and had consistently payed herself first, investing over 25 percent of her income each and every year into assets that have historically increased in value, although past performance is not a guarantee. (Individual blue-chip stocks, mutual funds, UITs, bullion, and even a few paintings.)

It turned out that she had built enough wealth that her portfolio was now generating over five times her current income needs. Rarely have I met a senior executive who has accomplished that feat. Turns out she was in a much better position than most of the executives that she ever worked for. To this day she continues to work, while living a very full and engaged life within her community, always assisting others in need, within her means.

ACCUMULATION ENHANCERS

In this section we will discuss four key enhancers that should assist you in the cause of becoming a better financial steward. They are as follows: deduct, defer, divert and convert.

Deduct: Making your investments tax deductible is a very powerful discipline. When dollars are invested into an IRA, a SEP, a 401(k), a 403(b), and other types of government-approved retirement plans, you may receive an immediate tax deduction. Based on your personal tax bracket, by investing in these programs, your current income tax will go down. Uncle Sam is, therefore, making a contribution for you.

Utilization of tax deferral is a concept you cannot afford to pass up. An individual in a 25 percent income tax bracket, investing $1,000 into an IRA, would otherwise only have $750 to invest. By utilizing the IRA, she has increased and leveraged her investment by 25 percent. By deferring that income tax she has retained control and accumulation opportunities on that 25 percent for many years, and a large percentage of the growth on that deferral will ultimately be hers after tax. This is a dramatic wealth-building technique, enhancing financial stewardship.

Defer: As introduced above, by deferring income taxes due into future years, you will receive a portion of the gain achieved due to that deferral. Whether the deferral is achieved via a qualified or a nonqualified investment, every year that you defer paying a tax, all things being equal, you have increased the opportunity of further accumulation by retaining a portion of that growth on the taxes that you deferred.

In a qualified investment such as an IRA or 401(k) or 403(b), deferring the tax can amount to an additional 25 to 30 percent of an entire portfolio. Deferring tax on nonqualified investments also works in a similar and valuable manner. However, do note that taxes will eventually be due upon withdrawal as withdrawn.

Divert: Another key strategy is to divert taxable income currently in high-income tax brackets into lower tax brackets, such as your children.

An added opportunity is that you may now be in position to help them understand the value of wealth accumulation and financial stewardship.

Convert: Another strategy is to convert assets currently paying ordinary income tax rates into investments that could receive the preferred capital gains, income tax rate treatment. Talk to your financial advisor about the opportunities you may have in mutual funds, individual stocks, real estate, and other areas that provide this special tax treatment for assets held for longer periods of time.

There are also advanced opportunities in the area of 1031 and 1035 tax-free exchanges that financial stewards should explore with their financial advisor.

STORY TIME: TIMELESS TALES OF ATHLETES, LOTTERY WINNERS, AND BENEFICIARIES OF SUBSTANTIAL WEALTH

Over the years I have been asked to help a number of professional athletes, lottery winners, and individuals who inherited substantial wealth. One area that I consistently provide caution is curbing the desire to become a great consumer of wealth. I help them enjoy their wealth while also understanding the value of becoming a first-generation wealth builder. Many have been given a great opportunity, and if they think as a business owner or first-generation wealth builder, the impact will dramatically enhance their future all the days of their lives.

All too often we read news stories reinforcing consumer tendencies of many professional athletes, lottery winners, and beneficiaries that quickly find themselves right back where they started. Their families did not go from rags to riches to rags over a period of generations; unfortunately they completed the wild, sad journey within a decade.

ACCUMULATION ADVERSARIES

There are many potholes in life; to be a lifelong, quality financial steward, one must stay constantly vigilant and cognizant of the classic adversaries to accumulation, which are taxation, inflation, poor judgment, and lack of protection.

Taxation: Due to our current tax code, as your accumulation grows, so will your potential income tax bracket. Quickly, individuals could find themselves in an effective 40 percent, or even higher, tax bracket. That is a heavy burden that slows even the best accumulation and wealth-preservation planning. Tax planning is a key to preserving wealth.

Inflation: Inflation is a mighty adversary. Money that is not invested in an effort to protect its purchasing power will be guaranteed to lose value, rendering it the equivalent of the change in your pocket or old postage stamps. Focusing on the inflation proofing of your portfolio is imperative.

Poor Judgment and Lack of Protection: These are the final two areas that often require the inclusion of a quality financial advisor to help individuals stay on track. While the true rate of return of an investment is not known until you subtract taxes and inflation, one must also remain vigilant to poor judgement and lack of protection.

Always strive to increase or maintain your purchasing power. Will Rogers once said, "Return *on* my investment is important, but return *of* my investment is imperative." A good financial steward would also require that their purchasing power is maintained or increased.

PROTECTION

The road of financial stewardship requires a solid foundation. It is very important for an individual to know they cannot build and preserve wealth without solid foundation. Making sure proper insurance is in place, covering your life, the effects of a long-term disability, and proper liability protection, is imperative. Your investments must also have realistic expectations and assurance that your risk tolerance is in line with your overall portfolio. These are all serious considerations that should also be discussed with your financial advisor.

STORY TIME: THE BIG BAD WOLF

We all know that if we build our house out of straw, we stand a great chance of it blowing away. If built out of sticks it may last a bit longer, but when the floodgates of life come our way, the house made of sticks will surely float away. That is why we must build our financial house on a solid foundation with solid brick. Ignoring a professional review of your financial affairs is just asking for one of the many big, bad wolves of life to blow your financial house down.

PHILANTHROPY AND LIFE PASSIONS

The essence of financial stewardship is to be a good steward of assets that will ultimately serve others. We can all do this by starting small. Even the largest foundations started small as the original donor thought like a first-generation accumulator.

- **The Call to Action:** Start with little steps, and be in alignment with your passion. Follow your passion; staying within these guidelines presented in this chapter will help you become a better steward of financial wealth.

- **Engage and utilize** your team of experts in the fields of law, accounting, and financial counselors. Just as you employ the counsel of a doctor, dentist, or clergy. The best always surround themselves with quality individuals.

- **Are you wise and fortunate in life?**

By acting as a quality financial steward in your daily endeavors, you will also be able to give generously to your life passions and assist those in need.

STORY TIME: THE CHEERFUL GIVER

I have had the pleasure to work with many CEOs as they lead some of America's greatest corporations. One who I found particularly enlightening was the CEO of one of America's largest corporations. He always carried himself in a truly peaceful way. When we finally met and began the review of all of his financials, I was taken aback a bit by the amount of his ongoing annual contributions to charity.

That really spoke volumes to me about his commitment to financial stewardship. I asked him how he came about the decision to be such a large and consistent charitable supporter. He said his commitment to stewardship started with his very first job. His parents were quite religious and believed in tithing as an expectation of a good steward. Even from his very first job, his parents requested that he give 10 percent of his earnings to someone else in need. He chose to continue that concept throughout his entire life.

Regardless of his income, he made sure to give to charity and other stewards caring for those in need. This gave him much to be thankful for, a peace and freeness to know others in areas of leadership were on his team helping those in need. He felt it was best to entrust and enable others close to the area of concern. While he may have the treasury, others had more time and the specific talent needed. He never saw the need for a private foundation; he just lived within his means, focused on serving others while accumulating wealth, and sharing what he could with those in need.

Story Time: Family Business, Family Values: Another family I had the honor of assisting owned a business that employed over one hundred employees. A sales organization; my client was the classic successful, first-generation owner. However, he was very concerned that his children did not embody the knowledge or desire to run the business. I asked if he thought his business was built on a solid foundation. He said, "What do you mean?" I said, "Aside from your son and daughter, you have several key salesmen who drive the vast majority of business.

"They are the keys to your clients and future profitability. What would happen should any of them leave for a variety of reasons, including new opportunities, bad health, family emergency, competitors, or a shift in business practices?" He had not considered the thought but with an open mind was willing to hear me out.

Unfortunately, in the ensuing years four of his key executives died unexpectedly. One from a heart attack, another to cancer, and then two separate car accidents claimed the lives of two additional key executives. Additionally, my client contracted cancer and died before retiring. His wife also passed shortly thereafter. All of this transpired within a period of fourteen months.

Fortunately the business did survive because he had restored the business to a solid foundation. We put in place key man protection and an estate liquidity plan that provided dollars for the next generation to withstand the many pressures of their new ownership, providing them the liquidity and personnel necessary to ensure the business's success and staying power. The business successfully transferred to the next generation. Because of their parents' planning, the next generation was now engaged as new, first-generation owners trying to grow the business as opposed to managing it.

ONE FINAL STORY—DON'T GET BURNT TO A CRISP

Reviewing the sage and well-known fable of the boiling frog, during a class in chemistry one day our professor had us set up a Bunsen burner under a small pail and then gave each of us a frog. (Unfortunately, this story does not end well for the frog.) What we did in class was put the frog into the pail and added some lukewarm water. All of our frogs moved around a bit, but none jumped out.

They all seemed to enjoy the lukewarm water. Then our professor asked us to turn up the heat in the Bunsen burner, and as expected, the temperature in the pail of water slowly increased. The frogs never felt the need to jump out. Instead they were enjoying the sauna. The water eventually began to bubble, and in the end all the frogs boiled to death, never leaving the pan of water.

The moral of the story our professor was trying to drive home was the need to be prepared for life's changes; we must never become complacent and always be prepared to take action when necessary. Are you complacent and in a cozy place? If so, enjoy, but please be prepared to jump. First-generation wealth builders and quality financial stewards are always preparing for and protecting the future of those they serve.

As we close this chapter, here are a few additional thoughts and principles for reflection:

- Know your mission and make it consist with your passion.
- Be a first-generation wealth builder.
- Take control of your destiny; when needed, be decisive.
- Do not harbor an entitlement attitude.
- Be a competent, educated risk taker.
- Focus on uncovering appreciating assets; resist excessive consumption.
- Always present yourself with integrity, engaging life in an ethical manner.

- Protect the purchasing power of your assets.
- In all financial endeavors, remember to: Plan, Execute and Review over and over.

I hope you found this chapter of value, as well as picked up a few new ideas and concepts to share with others, along with the motivation to increase and improve your family's wealth, health, and financial stewardship.

Professional Profile:
Douglas E. Knable, CLU, ChFC, CRPC
Doug.Knable@LFG.com | 724-940-6309 |
www.FamilyWealthGroup.com

Doug is able to share over thirty-five years of diverse financial planning services and experience with his clientele. As Chairman and CEO, Doug heads up the very seasoned and vibrant Family Wealth Management Group. Headquartered in Western Pennsylvania and with a clientele throughout America, FWMG has a full complement of registered representatives and dedicated staff focused on the Lincoln Financial Advisors "Serve First" philosophy.

At each confluence we put our client first, making sure that every solution is in the client's best interest and focused on the achievement of their goals and objectives. Listed below are just a few examples of Doug's passion and unfailing commitment to Family, Community, and Industry throughout his career:

- Chairman & CEO of Family Wealth Management Group, LLC
- Board of Trustees, Grove City College
- Planned Giving Steward, Ingomar United Methodist Church
- Top of the Table Member, MDRT
- Past Chairman & Lifetime Member, The Resource Group
- Emeritus Trustee & Past President, Community College of Allegheny County Educational Foundation
- Emeritus Member & Past Chairman of the Grove City College Alumni Council
- Long-term member, Estate Planning Council of Pittsburgh
- Long-term member, Society of Financial Service Professionals

Professional Profile:
Kelly L. Kennedy, CRPC®

Kelly.Kennedy@LFG.com | 724-940-6317 |

www.FamilyWealthGroup.com

Kelly joined Family Wealth Management Group, LLC (FWMG) in 2010, and after completing her advanced education working in Lincoln's National Planning Department, she quickly became an integral part of the overall FWMG team. Kelly analyzes clients' current investment- and estate-planning needs with a focus on achieving their goals and objectives while eliminating unnecessary risk and complexity. Kelly is committed to providing clarity and transparency with all of the clients she assists. Kelly holds FINRA Series 7 and 66 registrations, a Chartered Retirement Planning Consultant (CRPC®), and is a member of [1]MDRT (Million Dollar Round Table). She was named Lincoln's Pittsburgh transition [2]Planner of the Year in 2012.

Her industry and community involvement include:

- Board Member: [3]WISE Group (Women Inspiring Supporting Educating)
- Chair of the NextGen Committee within the WISE Group
- Board of Directors: Three Rivers Mothers' Milk Bank
- Leadership Council at Ingomar United Methodist Church
- President: Young Alumni Council at Miami University
- President: Pittsburgh Chapter of Miami University Alumni
- 2017 NACVA 40 Under Forty Honoree
  - http://www.nacva.com/40underforty

Being brought up in the family business, Kelly has often felt as though she's been in the business for over twenty-five years already. She lives in Wexford with her husband and two daughters.

CHAPTER THREE

FINANCIAL PLANNING FOR TODAY'S UNIQUE FAMILY

By Paula D. Tarpey

SECTION ONE: DEFINING TODAY'S FAMILY

There is no one definition of family today. There is a new version of the modern American Family.

We know from our own families and communities that today many Americans are single parents, and there are many same-sex or heterosexual couples who choose not to marry. In 2016, the Bureau of Labor Statistics reported that almost half of adults today do not live with a spouse. There are also young adults who live with their parents or grandparents, or blended families as a result of a second marriage.

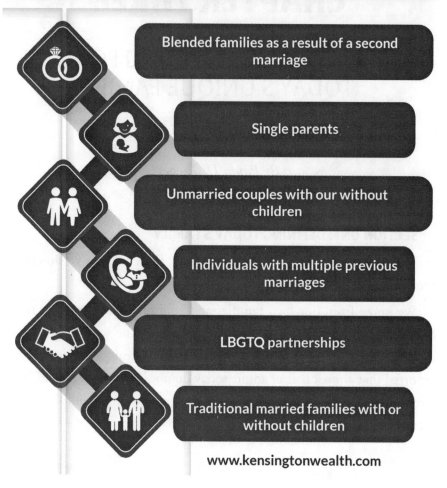

WHO IS TODAY'S FAMILY?

Blended families as a result of a second marriage

Single parents

Unmarried couples with our without children

Individuals with multiple previous marriages

LBGTQ partnerships

Traditional married families with or without children

www.kensingtonwealth.com

Another growing trend among many of our clients is that they have opened their doors to children now in their twenties, thirties, and forties that have experienced setbacks in life. Unemployment, divorce, unaffordable medical care, children with illness, and other issues are causing a number of young adults, who, a generation ago, would have struggled madly, to now seek aid from those who provided it best earlier in life.

The media, seemingly daily, shares the statistics and stories of our one-parent families and their potential financial challenges. According to a Pew Research Center analysis of recently released American Community Survey (ACS) and Decennial Census data, fewer than half of US kids younger than eighteen today are living in a home with two married, heterosexual parents in their first marriage. Four in every ten new marriages today involve remarriage.

Even in movies and entertainment we see the evolution of the traditional family. Television shows like *Modern Family* and *Parenthood* show the realities of what family means today. We all remember our old favorite shows like *Full House*, *The Brady Bunch*, or *Different Strokes* that also recognized the non-traditional family, even many years ago.

PLANNING FOR TODAY'S FAMILY

Why is planning important to these unique family structures? Well, frankly, planning is important to every family structure. In many ways, planning for these non-traditional families is no different than any other family. Planning is critical to achieve the vision you have for you and your family.

Planning is also especially important as laws and company benefits have not kept up with the change in family structure. Just as the laws surrounding same-sex marriage have recently changed, they could change again. Your use of planning and documents allows you to take control and leave as little to state law interpretation as possible. Overall, planning allows you to take responsibility for your modern family because nobody else is going to help you through this process.

UNIQUE CHALLENGES THAT REQUIRE THOUGHTFUL PLANNING

What are some unique challenges that require thoughtful planning? For non-married families, both same-sex and heterosexual families have challenges within areas of estate planning, income tax planning and retirement planning.

In estate planning, non-married couples do not have the same legal protection afforded to married spouses today. Additionally, they are not eligible for unlimited marital estate deduction as married couples are today. This means they don't have the ability to gift or transfer assets and ownership of assets without triggering taxation.

On income tax planning, non-married couples have more narrow tax brackets than married filers. This results in the fact that most non-married couples have a bigger income tax bill than married couples. Married couples with a large difference in incomes enjoy a marriage bonus, whereas married couples with higher dual incomes could see higher income taxes.

When it comes to retirement planning there are also specific challenges. Unmarried couples cannot contribute to spousal IRAs, and they are not able to treat inherited IRAs or qualified plans from their partner as their own. They must utilize a stretch strategy by withdrawing income over their life expectancy or pay a significant tax on any lump sum received through an inheritance. And today they must claim their own Social Security benefit; they are not eligible for spousal or survivor benefits under the Social Security system.

As an example, we have a client couple, John and Paige, living in an eastern state, who have lived together for over three decades and are unmarried. This particular couple is a high net-worth couple who own multiple homes together.

Under current law, John is not eligible for survivor benefits from Paige's government pension, and Paige will not receive a survivor benefit from John's Social Security. Proper planning is essential to mitigate these deficiencies.

YOUR PLANNING TEAM

Who should be on your planning team to help you take action in the areas you have identified? Your financial planner is typically your quarterback to help you identify your goals, detail your current situation and identify actions, and most importantly help you take action to get it done. Obviously you also need help from your estate attorney and your accountant.

Specifically, your estate attorney is going to be responsible for drafting the estate documents to put your words into action. Consider involving adult children in the planning process, as some of it may clearly involve them. The more your family is aware of your intent, the smoother your planning will go.

SECTION TWO: ACCOUNT TITLING AND CO-MINGLING OF ASSETS AND DEBTS FOR UNMARRIED COUPLES OR SECOND MARRIAGES

For many couples who choose not to marry or for couples who have just entered into a second marriage, discussion of financial matters starts with candid discussion. Both parties of the couple come to the conversation with different backgrounds, they were raised by different parents, they have different feelings about money and debt, and, consequently, their feelings about financial matters will differ.

Any financial conversation should start very candidly. You should discuss your attitude toward money; determine where you agree and where you differ. Looking at the big picture, it is important that the two of you determine what type of lifestyle you want together. For example, is a vacation home important to one? Is travel important to another? How do you feel about debt? Or carrying a mortgage into retirement?

We find in our financial planning practice when we are counseling with a couple, unmarried or not, many have very different views when it comes to a mortgage. If they were raised by a family who felt it was very important to pay off their mortgage before retirement, that is an objective that is equally important to them today.

If both partners are working outside of the home, it is important to know how to manage day-to-day cash needs. Do you contribute equally or by some percentage of income earned? Do you maintain a joint checking account or have separate accounts?

For second marriages, how does the non-birth parent share in the expenses of children? It is important to talk about these issues up front so they do not cause miscommunication or disagreement later down the road. However, we believe one key decision to be made early in your relationship is whether to combine your finances or continue to manage them separately.

Note that, as we alluded to earlier, though, unmarried couples have less legal protection. If you combine your finances and your relationship ends, there are few legal guidelines to help you unravel your comingled assets.

OPTIONS FOR TITLING OF ASSETS

Titling of assets is a key financial aspect for any couple. Let's explore some options for titling of assets. However, it should be known that these options vary by state. These options should be explored by an attorney who is reviewing your assets and objectives.

Your options for titling would include owning assets separately, owning assets jointly with rights of survivorship, or jointly as tenants in common. Jointly with rights of survivorship titling provides you both with the ability to access all of the account at any time. You could also title your assets in a revocable living trust, although practically speaking, this can be cumbersome.

One other option available in many states is to own separate property with a transfer of death or payable on death provision. These allow the transfer of your separate property to your partner upon your death and avoid probate. However, as noted, TOD or POD options are not available in every state.

THE ISSUE OF DEBT

Another key financial issue is debt. If you are an unmarried couple, living together does not make you responsible for your partner's debts. However, if you choose to share debt obligations remember one rule, that with shared credit and shared debt come shared liability. Most debt is considered joint and severable, which means that either party is responsible for the entire debt. One other consideration is that individual credit ratings will reflect on each if you decide to share credit.

One practical solution for titling and other issues faced by unmarried couples is to enter into a cohabitation agreement. A cohabitation agreement, similar to a prenuptial agreement for married couples, is simply a contract that states how you plan to share assets, debts, and any property you have now or in the future.

It outlines the legal and forcible terms of your arrangement, which sets out in advance conditions for terminating or making changes to the agreement. This avoids any surprises or expectations and provides you with an opportunity to know your partner a little better.

You and your partner should start by drafting a checklist of all the possible issues. Make sure to include expectations of support or inheritance and what to do in the event of an emergency. Discussing the contract can be a great way to explore some difficult ideas about responsibility and commitment and how these manifest materially.

Once you have established a list of issues and how you would address them, you need to consult with an attorney in your area. When interviewing attorneys, do not hesitate to ask the attorney what charge would be applied to draft such an agreement, and make sure they have a good understanding of your needs.

SECTION THREE: NAMING BENEFICIARIES ON YOUR ACCOUNTS

For the modern family, beneficiary designations are a very important tool. Beneficiary designations are the least expensive way to designate who is to receive certain assets; actually it is free. Specifically, IRAs, annuities, life insurance, and qualified retirement accounts have named beneficiaries.

You can name anyone you choose to be a beneficiary of your account. When you name a beneficiary, the assets will go to whom you choose and the assets bypass other estate documents like a will or trust and will also avoid probate. If you have no beneficiary named, the asset becomes part of your probate estate, and your estate documents or state law will determine who receives that asset.

One of the most flexible provisions of naming beneficiaries is that it is changeable. You can change a beneficiary designation as many times as you choose between today and the day you pass. Single parents, second marriages, and unmarried couples all have certain issues involving beneficiaries.

SINGLE PARENTS

Beneficiary designation should be a big concern to single parents with young children. Minor children are not allowed to own or manage an asset; that is, children under eighteen years of age should not be the beneficiary of your assets.

However, as every single parent needs to determine who would care for their children if something happened to them, that same person may not be the same person who would be responsible for managing assets on your children's behalf. In other words, your preferred guardian may not be your preferred money manager.

Unless you make proper provisions today for your beneficiary designations, the probate court could take over management of your assets for the benefit of your children until your child becomes an adult. Then, in most states once those same children are eighteen without a trust as a beneficiary, there is no control of the assets if you pass. And even the best-intentioned eighteen year old could blow through the money.

One of the best choices for the beneficiary designation for your minor children is to consider setting up a trust. This trust, which would only come to be at your passing, would name a custodian for your assets for the benefit of your children. This trust could be customized to allow the trustee to provide assets for your children for the benefit of their health, maintenance, education, and welfare and could also preserve these assets for their long-term use.

You should know if you have children with special needs, they may need a specific special needs trust to provide for them. Their issues are unique as they have certain parameters regarding qualifying for governmental aid. Make sure your attorney, who might draft this type of trust document, is aware of the special challenges with special needs children.

SECOND MARRIAGES

Naming beneficiaries in second-marriage situations has its own unique challenges. Many partners in second marriages want to take care of their new spouse for their lifetime but want their assets to ultimately pass to their children of their previous marriage.

Another concern for a spouse in a second marriage is that divorce from their first spouse does not prevent unattended beneficiaries. As an example, we had a client who had divorced his first wife many years earlier and was remarried to Stephanie in Arizona. Unfortunately, David was struck with cancer and died prematurely. He had never named a new beneficiary on his 401(k) through his employer.

The beneficiary designation on his 401(k) was still his first wife. The courts ruled in this case that divorce did not prevent the unintended beneficiary, and his first wife did receive the assets as a beneficiary of the 401(k) account. The Supreme Court of the United States has affirmed this in additional case law.

Another key question for couples in a second marriage is how do you recognize the passing of a birth parent should they pass before their stepparent? How do you recognize their passing to their kids if the second spouse retains all the assets until they pass? Again, this is a special circumstance where a trust could be very helpful in solving this need.

Spouses in a second marriage could consider naming a trust as beneficiary of their life insurance. This trust could be established to provide for the surviving spouse until their passing, whereby the remaining assets are then passed to the children of the first marriage.

Insurance can be a helpful tool to provide some inheritance to the passing of their first birth parent. If using life insurance to solve this need, make sure to use permanent life insurance product to assure that the coverage will be there whenever needed. Term insurance cannot be relied upon, as it is never assured that the person will die during the term of the policy.

A specific provision within a will that addresses some of these beneficiary concerns is called a QTIP Provision. QTIP is an abbreviation for Qualified Terminable Interest Property. How does a QTIP work to control property?

When the first spouse dies, the survivor gets what is called a "life estate" in the assets that are left to the QTIP trust. The survivor is entitled to any income the assets of the trust produce, and in the case of real estate, the survivor is entitled to its use. Only a surviving spouse can be named as the life beneficiary. The survivor does not, however, have full ownership of the trust assets and cannot sell them or give them away.

The QTIP trust can establish very broad provisions for their use. Again, the surviving spouse can use these assets for their health, maintenance, education, welfare, using income, and/or principal for their use for the rest of their life.

When the second spouse dies, QTIP trust assets go to the final beneficiary named in the trust. Commonly, the final beneficiaries are children from the other spouse's previous marriage.

Each spouse that is a party to a second marriage can set up a QTIP trust leaving assets to the other interest. Though somewhat complex in nature, a QTIP trust is considered an important component of any estate plan.

UNMARRIED COUPLES

There are two main issues for unmarried couples with beneficiary designations. Specifically, if no beneficiary is named on an account, a surviving spouse is generally what is considered the default beneficiary. An unmarried partner will not be the default beneficiary. This is why beneficiary forms and designations for unmarried couples are even more important.

The second significant issue for unmarried couples is that beneficiary designations to their partners do not defer income tax liability. Beneficiary designations to a surviving spouse of IRAs and retirement assets to each other at death, do defer income tax liability. Unmarried beneficiaries face immediate taxation and other tax implications of leaving retirement assets to someone who is not your spouse.

SECTION FOUR: SOCIAL SECURITY

UNMARRIED COUPLES

Adults who live together but are not married are not eligible for their partner's survivor's retirement or Social Security benefit. This is true even if their children are dependents of both. Marriage benefits from Social Security can be substantial, especially when a couple has a large disparity in earnings. A non-working spouse may receive up to half of the primary breadwinner's Social Security benefit as a spousal benefit.

There are several solutions for unmarried couples in this situation. If one partner stays home to take care of the home and children, the other partner could employ them and they would thus earn their own Social Security credits. Taxes and FICA would be paid on the wages and in some states there would be other costs and taxes, but it is worth exploring, particularly if the stay-at-home partner just needs a few more credits to be eligible for their own Social Security benefit.

Another solution may be available if either partner had been married before. If either partner had been in a marriage previously, they could potentially get benefits from an ex-spouse's Social Security if their prior marriage lasted ten years. This includes retirement and survivor Social Security benefits. The key to this is the ten-year-marriage requirement.

It should be noted, to begin collecting retirement Social Security benefits from an ex-spouse, the ex-spouse has to have filed for their own Social Security retirement benefit.

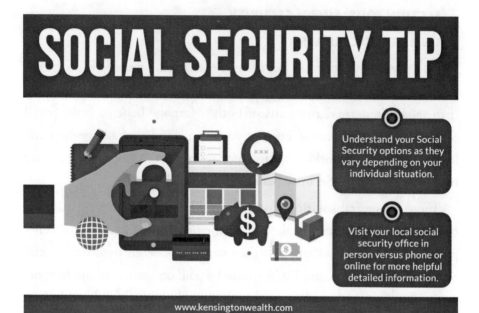

For advice on how best to maximize your Social Security benefits, contact your local Social Security administration office. As a financial planner I recommend an in-person visit to the Social Security administration office, as these associates tend to be more helpful when you are talking to them in person verses talking to them on the phone or visiting the Social Security Administration website.

SAME-SEX MARRIED COUPLES

The US Department of Justice ruling in August 2015 treats married same-sex couples equally across the country when determining eligibility for Social Security benefits. However, there is a potential problem for same-sex couples wanting to claim Social Security benefits and meeting the marriage duration requirement if they recently married and live in former non-recognition states. This could result in some couples being denied Social Security spousal benefits.

SECTION FIVE: CORPORATE BENEFITS AND PENSION ELECTION OPTIONS

UNMARRIED COUPLES

When many employers offered domestic partner benefits, it was because same-sex couples could not get married. Under current law, as same-sex partners won the right to marry, some employers are dropping their domestic partner coverage. If you are not married, you may or may not have the option of adding your partner to your corporate health benefit or your corporate pension benefits to get a joint and survivor monthly retirement benefit.

If a single-life retirement pension benefit is all that is available to you, consider using life insurance to re-inherit your partner for those possible pension benefits if you pass before they do. Again, in this instance make sure to use permanent life insurance products like Universal Life or Variable Universal Life so that it fits your long-term planning needs that may not be met through traditional term insurance.

Many same-sex couples did not choose joint and survivor benefits, as they were not able to when they elected their pension benefit. If you are already receiving your pension and are now married or will soon be married to your same-sex partner, look into whether your pension has reversion rights.

Reversion rights allow the pensioner the ability to change their pension election after they originally elected a single-life pension. This reversion provision could also apply to single parents who are looking to remarry, or divorced or widowed couples looking to remarry.

This reversion could also work in reverse and allow a widow or widower the choice to revert from the original, joint-pension election to a single-life pension election upon the passing of their spouse. This would provide a higher lifetime pension to the now-single partner.

It should be noted that pension benefits are considered a joint asset if earned during a marriage, therefore divorced parents may be sharing some of their pension benefits with an ex-spouse even if remarried.

SUMMARY

While every family needs to plan for their financial future, the changing picture of today's family provides unique opportunities for planning. Proper planning ensures that you exert the most control on your financial future for today and at your passing. Proper planning seeks to optimize future income streams like a pension or Social Security and reduce tax or probate costs. Don't let inaction impact the financial security of your family or leave you vulnerable to ever-changing laws.

The first step is clear communication with your unique family and your planning team. Your planning team, including your financial planner, estate attorney, and adult children should help you make your financial vision a reality.

Professional Profile:
Paula D. Tarpey

Paula.Tarpey@LFG.com | 614-431-4338 |
www.KensingtonWealth.com

As partner and Chief Operating Officer at Kensington Wealth Partners, Ltd., Paula Tarpey focuses on the implementation of strategies for wealth accumulation, preservation, and transfer. In her two decades of serving clients, she ensures that all clients' financial plan objectives are met. She cares about each client and takes personal responsibility for their financial well-being.

Tarpey has been honored with national speaking engagements on the topics of financial planning case design, charitable giving techniques, and practice management. Prior to joining Kensington Wealth, Tarpey worked in commercial, private, and investment banking, using this prior experience as greater breadth and depth for the benefit of all she serves.

Tarpey received a bachelor's degree in Finance from Miami University in Oxford, Ohio. She holds the Series 7 securities registration through the Financial Industry Regulatory Authority (FINRA). Tarpey is married, has two children, and lives in Lewis Center, Ohio. She serves her community through her work with the Delaware County Foundation and Women Giving Together. She also has two rescue dogs, and in her free time she enjoys fitness training, watching sports, and spending time with family and friends.

CHAPTER FOUR

ADVANCED PLANNING FOR SENIOR EXECUTIVES

By Paul A. Gydosh, Jr

THE OPPORTUNITY: INDEPENDENCE!

You have reached success by almost every measure.

An amazing amount of hard work, study, long hours, drive, and purpose on your part has resulted in the most senior of positions leading your organization. You should be able to kick back, take a breath, and enjoy the fruits of your labor.

What is it that keeps nagging at you? What is it that is there just under the surface—that question, that concern, that anxiety? Do I have enough? Are we financially independent? Could I retire or try something new if I wanted to? If you have asked this question of yourself, you are not alone.

BETTER MANAGER/LEADER

Knowing you do not have to work is liberating; it is freedom! Freedom to share your true input on business issues and not be concerned with political backlash and implications—without career repercussions. Your true self is what your business wanted when they hired you.

Have you seen how your CEO or other CEOs seem so much more open, forthright, warm, and self-assured? Sure, the position is part of it. Financial independence is the other.

Are you the one who everyone turns to with their personal financial questions? Or are you the one going down the hall, closing the door of a peer, and asking their opinion or advice on your benefits, stock options, pensions, or retirement?

How is it that Sam, who has risen to the same lofty level in your organization, seems to have it all together with a lake house and retirement planned at a young age and with no mortgage? Why him—and not me?

Financial independence flows from understanding cash flow, equity; needs versus wants; and action.

BETTER SPOUSE/PARTNER

Have you ever had a fight with your spouse about money? Have you ever felt insecure or less than genuine when you have told others that your financial future is under control? Do you know, actually know *analytically*, where you stand *today* on retirement and financial independence?

Are you capturing enough of the many dollars that flow through your hands? And are you on track to walking away from the high pressure corporate world at age fifty, fifty-five, sixty, or whatever age you have in mind?

In the book, *The Number* by Lee Eisenberg, he focuses on calculating the one number you need to have accumulated by your target age to be financially independent the rest of your life. What I like about the book and its key concept is that it is simple. When it comes to behavioral economics, simple is powerful. I suggest you obtain a copy of the book and read it, and let me know what you think. Email me at paul.gydosh@ kensingtonwealth.com.

TIME AND EMOTIONAL DRAIN

How much do you worry about being prepared? What do you feel and think when you receive your quarterly 401(k) statement? Is it comfort or anxiety? Or worse, do you ignore it because there is no use in worrying?

Do money arguments at home create a stress that just adds to that of your job, your boss, your direct reports, and all those who want your job?

Take Control

Just as you attack problems, issues, and opportunities in your day job, do the same in your financial life. Read on to learn how.

Your world *expects* you to know everything.

But you don't. We understand. Your job is to be an expert in your area of business and in your industry. Life is a multivariable equation. It's complicated.

You use outside specialists in many elements of your life. You hire a doctor to help you determine the cause of an illness, to give you a subjective observation of that, and identify an action, which can be a change in habits or taking some medicine to fix the problem. You hire an attorney for his or her counsel and recommended action. Use a financial planner in the same way.

APPLES, BANANAS, ORANGES AND MORE

Not only are you tasked with all of the jargon of your industry, but the executive benefits area has its own jargon that requires a significant amount of time and energy to understand. Let your planner help you through this alphabet soup of executive benefits so that your understanding will rise, your comfort will grow, and you will make better decisions about your financial future.

WHEN IS A DOLLAR NOT A DOLLAR?

Many of us feel confident and almost cocky about the balances in our 401(k) accounts. It is sobering to many when they are reminded that the federal and state governments own a significant portion of these balances.

It is called ordinary income taxes. Ordinary income tax rates are low from a historical perspective but approach 50 percent for many senior executives. These ordinary income tax rates do change from time to time depending on the current administration and lawmakers in Washington, D.C.

Elements that affect the withdrawal of qualified money, that is 401(k) and IRA dollars, include your incremental marginal tax rate. That is the rate applied to the last dollar earned or withdrawn in a given year. It is your highest rate of taxation. Your effective rate is really the average rate of taxes paid. It is determined by taking the total taxes paid in a year and dividing it by the total earned income and withdrawn IRA or 401(k) dollars.

Minimizing taxes paid helps us get to our financial independence goals quicker or requires fewer dollars to be withdrawn from our accounts while in retirement to meet our spending needs. It also permits a higher net investment return with no additional risk.

Other elements that cause a dollar to not necessarily equal a dollar include vesting schedules on restricted stock units, for example, and profit-sharing plans. They may also include forfeiture clauses. A professional planner slows this all down. He or she takes the mystery out of all of these pieces and parts and helps create a clean, clear picture on an apples-to-apples basis of where you are today. We use graphics and executive summaries as well as cash flow and present value analysis.

TOMORROW'S PICTURE: MY VISION

This is the fun part. Your planner is interested, engaged, and excited to learn what you have envisioned for your future. What lifestyle do you want? Where do you intend to live? Are you going to maintain your primary residence as it is today and live a portion of the year in a resort area?

Do you intend to go on medical or church missions to a third-world area? Are you going to go back to school to get that second degree that you always wanted? Or are you going to be a pest to your children and grandchildren? All of this requires some assured cash flow. And it requires a target age and maybe a backup age if that target age is pretty aggressive.

SPOUSAL/PARTNER AGREEMENT AND OWNERSHIP

In effective planning, both partners need to be on board. As cash flows through your hands as regular salary and bonuses are received, or distributions are made from the business, you have to have taken ownership of The Plan as your filter for money decision making.

So the most recent bonus just arrived and the question is, does that money go to the "fund your retirement at fifty-eight" goal, or are we doing the second trip to Europe this year? Are we adding on to the vacation home at the lake?

Other opportunities for uses of money include: Do we accelerate the pay down or payoff of our mortgage? Do we pay all or a portion of our children's (or grandchildren's) college costs? Do we step in and help our parents in their retirement? Typically, we find that our clients have achieved more financial success than their siblings, so they help more. Do I buy that 1965 GTO or Ford Cobra that I always wanted when I was young?

Add your unique wants, needs, and obligations to the list. They all pull at your money and your bigger goals.

Prioritizing these key goals is so critical to achieving them. You know that in business it is determining the goals, quantifying the goals, and then prioritizing the goals that lead to success. The same holds true in your private life. Some of the goals can be stretch goals. That's good! Outrageous goals . . . well, I'll leave that to you!

RISK MANAGEMENT—WHERE ARE THE SINKHOLES?

Big Mistake or Little Mistake?

At this point in your life and career, it is really all about big mistakes verses little mistakes. A small mistake would be picking the wrong stock mutual fund manager. Advertising in the financial world would lead you to believe that the superstar manager is the most important decision one could make in their financial future. That is not the case.

It is true that a better manager or a better fund could incrementally improve one's account performance over some period of time, but the lion's share of investment performance is driven by asset allocation. A *big mistake* in your life is assuming that maximum funding my 401(k) and holding all my shares of my company stock will get me to retirement in proper shape.

It is likely that the lifestyle that you are living today and intend to live once retired require much more funding than that which could come from the maximum funding of your 401(k). It is also likely that no diversification from a very concentrated stock position in your own company stock may catch up with you at some point between now and when it really matters.

Just ask those in Silicon Valley in the years 2000, 2001, and 2002 what happened to their net worth and financial independence goals when the tech boom went bust. That is not say that allowing a significant number of shares of one's company stock to accumulate is a bad thing. Look at the Microsoft millionaires as an example.

Ask those who loaded up on real estate in the early and mid-years of the first decade of the twenty-first century. Not only did the equity/stock markets drop dramatically in concert, but all real estate took a major hit to valuations. Our home values dropped—a lot. Not an issue if you didn't intend to move, but a big issue if your company transferred you, a headhunter called with a great offer across the country, or you simply wanted to refinance.

Institutional real estate took quite a hit. Resort or vacation property values dropped 50 percent and more. Markets such as south Florida, the Jersey Shore, and Las Vegas suffered greatly, as did senior executives who had bought just a few short years before.

This is where a professional can play a key role by analytically helping one understand the value of monetizing some of those shares of stock to assure financial independence and some of your other life goals.

Another big mistake to avoid is not protecting your income against a long-term disability. If retirement is imminent, this is no longer necessary. However, if you are a number of years from that point, you must act now to protect your most valuable asset, which is your ability to earn a significant income. The smaller mistake would be laboring over one disability insurance company verses another. Just go out and secure the coverage. Gain the insight of your financial professional here.

HEDGING AND DIVERSIFICATION

If you have a highly concentrated position in your company stock, learn and use strategies to mitigate that investment risk. Your financial planner can help identify the risk, quantify how much is necessary to assure financial independence, and then educate on various strategies which include put options, call options, zero cost collars (combining puts and calls to create a defined floor and ceiling for potential gain or loss), diversification, 10b5-1 rules, and margin loans. See a later section of this chapter for more information on some of these strategies.

TAX TREATMENT DIVERSIFICATION

If you are like most senior executives of large corporations and organizations, you tend to accumulate very, very large balances in your qualified plans. These are typically 401(k)s and 403(b)s. The upside of that accumulation, beyond the balance itself, is the tax deduction that the government provided when you made the original deposit as well as the tax-deferred growth.

As we learned earlier, however, the government really owns a portion of your balance because each dollar will be fully taxed at your highest marginal rate when you withdraw the funds in retirement. As a result, it is prudent to accumulate funds in other forms of investment. It is prudent because tax laws will change.

Ask yourself, "Will the government need more or less money to operate five years from now?" Of course they will need more tax revenues. Where do you think they will go to get those dollars? You are very much in their sweet spot.

When Elliott Ness and the G-Men asked Willie Sutton, the famous criminal, why he robbed banks, he replied, "Because that is where the money is." Congress, when asked five, ten, and fifteen years from now with funding an ever-increasing operating cost, will look to where the money is. There are trillions and trillions of dollars sitting in 401(k) s, deferred compensation plans, profit sharing plans, and other pretax programs.

You are in the crosshairs of government tax increases. Let's be smart today. Your planning professional can help you identify and then fund multiple types of accounts that provide varying tax treatment as a way to diversify in the tax dimension.

UNDERSTANDING FINANCIAL INSTRUMENTS AND TECHNIQUES

OPTION PLANS

- **ISOs**

  o Incentive Stock Options (ISOs) are a type of <u>employee stock option</u> that can be granted only to employees and confer a <u>US tax benefit</u>. ISOs are also sometimes referred to as incentive share options or Qualified Stock Options by the <u>IRS</u>.

  o The tax benefit is that at exercise the individual does not have to pay ordinary income tax (or employment taxes) on the difference between the exercise price and the fair market value of the shares issued (however, the holder may have to pay US <u>alternative minimum tax</u> instead). Instead, if the shares are held for one year from the date of exercise and two years from the date of grant, then the profit (if any) made on sale of the shares is taxed as a long-term capital gain. Long-term capital gain is taxed in the US at lower rates than ordinary income.

- **Non-Qualified**

  o Non-Qualified Stock Options (typically abbreviated NSO or NQSO) are a form of compensation that is designed to align the interests of the executive with that of the shareholder.

  o They typically include a vesting schedule. Non-qualified stock options result in additional taxable income to the recipient at the time that they are exercised, the amount being the difference between the exercise price and the market value on that date. The tax treatment is that of ordinary income.

- **SARs**

  o Stock Appreciation Rights (SARs) is a method for companies to give their management or employees a bonus if the company performs well financially. SARs resemble employee stock options in that the holder/employee benefits from an increase in stock price.

- **RSUs**

  o Restricted Stock Unit (RSUs) are grants valued in terms of company stock, but company stock is not issued at the time of the grant. After the recipient of a unit satisfies the vesting requirement, the company distributes shares or the cash equivalent of the number of shares used to value the unit.

  o They are assigned a fair market value when they vest. Upon vesting, they are considered income and a portion of the shares are withheld to pay income taxes. The employee receives the remaining shares and can sell them at any time.

THE SUPPLEMENTAL RETIREMENT PLANS

- **NQDC**

  o A Non-Qualified Deferred Compensation (NQDC) plan is an elective or non-elective plan, agreement, method, or arrangement between an employer and an executive to pay the employee/executive compensation in the future.

  o If your employer offers a NQDC plan, you might want to explore this option. NQDC plans allow executives to defer a much larger portion of their compensation and to defer taxes on the money until the deferred funds are withdrawn.

- **Phantom Stock**

  o Phantom Stock is a contractual agreement between a corporation and recipients of *phantom* shares that bestow upon the grantee the right to a cash payment at a designated time or in association with a designated event in the future, which payment is to be in an amount tied to the market value of an equivalent number of company shares.

- **SERPs**
  - o Supplemental Executive Retirement Plan (SERP) is a deferred compensation agreement between the company and the key executive, whereby the company agrees to provide supplemental retirement income to the executive and his family if certain pre-agreed eligibility and vesting conditions are met by the executive.

- **Cash Balance Pensions**
  - o A defined benefit plan that specifies both the contribution to be credited to each participant and the investment earnings to be credited based on those contributions. Each participant has an account that resembles those in a 401(k) or profit-sharing plan. Through a well-designed integration of your 401(k) and CB plan, as much as $263,000 of salary and bonus income can be tax deferred.

RISK MANAGEMENT TOOLS

- **Puts and Calls**
  - o A call is the right to buy stock for a given price within a given period of time, while a put is the right to sell a stock for a given price within a given period of time. The price at which the option can be exercised—in other words, the price at which the stock may be bought or sold—is known as the strike price. Puts are sometimes used by executives to provide some downside protection to monetary value of a concentrated company stock position.

- **Margin Loans**
  - o Your brokerage firm can lend you money against the value of certain stocks, bonds, and mutual funds in your portfolio. That borrowed money is called a margin loan. A margin loan can be a

valuable tool in the right circumstances, but be aware that it can magnify both profits and losses.

o Typically, an executive is permitted to borrow up to 50 percent of their non-IRA, non-401(k) stock and mutual-fund values. This is usually at favorable borrowing rates and does not trigger taxation.

SELLING/TRADING

- **Cashless Option Exercises**

    o A transaction that is used when exercising employee stock options (ESO). Essentially, what you do here is borrow enough money from your broker to exercise your stock options without providing any cash for the transaction. The brokerage firm is fully repaid for the temporary loan through the proceeds of the sale. This is essentially a simultaneous transaction.

- **10b5-1 Insider Trading Plans**

    o Rule 10b5-1 is established by the Securities & Exchange Commission (SEC) to allow insiders of publicly traded corporations to set up a trading plan for selling stocks they own. Rule 10b5-1 allows major holders to sell a predetermined number of shares at a predetermined time. Many corporate executives use 10b5-1 plans to avoid accusations of insider trading and to permit scheduled sales to occur even during blackout periods.

FOCUS ON YOU!

Treat Your Personal Financial Well-Being like a Business

Let's attack your personal financial well-being the way you have your career. This deserves your study, education, and learning. Hire professionals. Pay your planning professional a fee. Pay it again next year and each succeeding year. How many times have we read that most couples spend more time (and money) planning for their next vacation than they do for their financial well-being?

Once you have a plan in place, monitor your results. Adjust as you go, just as you do in the corporate or not-for-profit world. Change your tactics when you change your plan or your goals. Set one- and three-year and lifetime goals. We suggest scheduling a short time weekly or monthly to focus on personal finance just as you do your personal fitness. Block that time out in Outlook or your Day-Timer.

PAY FOR HELP

Your employer may offer financial planning fee reimbursement. If so, take advantage of it. Do this today. This will benefit you, your spouse/partner, and your family for decades to come. If planning is not paid as a perk in your organization, pay for it yourself. Take ownership of your personal financial well-being and take responsibility. It is that important.

ACT NOW!

There will never be the perfect time for personal financial planning. There is always a crisis at the office. There is always that new business opportunity and the excitement to go along with it. There is always that new competitor who is digging into your market share, and you have to do something about it right now. There is always something at home, good or bad, that seems to take priority.

Do not let that happen. Do this planning now. The sooner you start, the easier it will be to accomplish your personal and family financial goals.

Get your spouse or partner involved from the beginning. Do not do it all and then tell them the result. To do so invites a breakdown during implementation, the action period.

Where did the last ten years go? The next ten will go by even faster. The magic of compounding and the time value of money fully support acting sooner for a much bigger and better result and the sense of security that results.

SPOUSE/PARTNER

As we opened this chapter, we touched on the success that you have experienced in much of your life. People look to you for guidance and answers. Your spouse or partner probably does the same. They might presume that your personal financial house is in order.

What we have found over the many years in working so intimately with our clients is that many spouses have an unspoken anxiety over their financial condition. Professional planning, when done as a couple, will address this head on. Both of you will experience a thorough understanding of where you are today, what is necessary to get to where you want to be, the priority over those very specific actions to be taken, and finally, direct control over the outcome. This is liberating and empowering.

FAMILY

Our children watch what we do—and they watch how we act. I am not so sure that our children take advice that we share with them as much as monitor what they see. It has a lifelong impact on them. The example you set by planning for your financial future will bias them to do the same and to do it sooner in life than you did.

How many people have you heard say, "I wish I had started saving for retirement sooner"? Or, "I wish I had started funding my 401(k) earlier in my career." Or, "I wish I knew then what I know now." This applies directly to our opportunity for financial independence and to theirs. Leave them a better financial legacy.

COMMUNITY

You may be active in your community and charity today in terms of giving your time, expertise, energy, and even money. True financial independence enables those who want to support their community and their charity to do even more. The leverage that this can provide and its impact on so, so many others is very powerful. But it has to start with knowing, truly knowing, where you stand financially before you can step in and help others.

Financial independence sets you free!

Professional Profile:
Paul A. Gydosh, Jr. CFP®, CRPC®

Paul.Gydosh@LFG.com | 614-431-4336 |

www.KensingtonWealth.com

As the Managing Director of Kensington Wealth Partners, Ltd., Paul provides counseling and implementation strategies for wealth preservation, growth, and transfer and leads a national planning and investment advisory firm he founded thirty years ago. His clients include successful individuals, families, professionals, business owners, and executives of private and public enterprises as well as foundations and trusts.

Paul has been listed in WORTH Magazine as one of the top 250 financial advisors in America in multiple years. Business First of Columbus has listed him among its Top Financial Planners every year since 2001.

He is a co-author of the book, *Giving: Philanthropy for Everyone.* He has written numerous published articles on advanced estate planning and is a frequent lecturer, nationally, on the subjects of finance, serious investing, and charitable giving.

Paul received a Master's in Business Administration from the Fuqua School of Business at Duke University in Durham, North Carolina. He also received a bachelor's degree in Electrical Engineering from Ohio University in Athens, Ohio.

Paul's community involvement, past and present, includes: Trustee of the Ohio University Foundation, Chairman of the Mayor's Advisory Council on Voluntary Services (Columbus), Rock and Roll Hall of Fame Advisory Board Member, Adjunct Professor of Finance Franklin University, National Board Chairman of The Resource Group, President of Dublin AM Rotary, Ohio University Russ College of Engineering Board of Visitors, President of the Duke Club of Central Ohio, Caring Program for Children Board Member, COSI Community Board Member and Endowment Committee Chair, and others.

Paul, a licensed pilot, is married, with two grown daughters, and lives in Powell, Ohio.

CHAPTER FIVE

GENERATIONAL WEALTH PLANNING

By Craig C. Bartlett

GENERATIONAL WEALTH PLANNING DEFINED—YOU ARE NOT ALONE

You have prepared your wealth for your family . . . but have you prepared your family for your wealth?

You have spent a lifetime creating, growing, preserving, and protecting your wealth. You have ensured that you and your spouse are financially secure and that potential risks to your security have been addressed. You also have determined how your wealth will be distributed upon your death, but that is just the first step.

Like any responsible parent you want your children and grandchildren to learn the importance of personal initiative, hard work, and social responsibility. Are you concerned that inheriting money may become a disincentive to their self-motivation, productivity, and achievement?

You are not alone! You may personally know wealthy families whose descendants inherit significant wealth and become unmotivated, unproductive spendthrifts who eventually squander their inheritance. It is often referred to as "shirt sleeves to shirt sleeves."

You can take some simple steps to help ensure this does not happen to your family, your vision, and your wealth. It starts with engaging your children and family members in an open, meaningful conversation; one that is not about money but rather focuses on your family's mission and philosophy. After all, your valuables are only part of your legacy.

Passing down your values will help ensure that future generations understand and appreciate that while money brings advantages, it also is tempered with the obligations and responsibilities that you instill in your descendants. Proactive generational wealth planning will help future generations appreciate what it took you to build and maintain your wealth, embrace your values and beliefs, and ultimately become outstanding stewards of those values and beliefs, not just your money.

If you agree it is time to build a generational wealth plan, you will derive much value from this chapter to ensure that you are helping and not hurting as your wealth cascades down to the next generation, and hopefully multiple generations. For you to gain the most, it will be important to internalize the Action Questions posed, request your Free Gifts by sending an email to <u>WBD@LFG.com,</u> and learn from others' failures and successes.

Action Question: What are you doing on a proactive basis to increase the probability that your children and grandchildren will be outstanding stewards of your wealth, not just your money?

Client Situation: When asked this question to a client their immediate reaction was like a deer in the headlights as they quickly grew uncertain as to the true impact as well as mental and financial readiness their children had to accept the inheritance they were preparing. It clearly demonstrated the need for a family meeting and open discussion to begin educating them on what to expect and how to handle it.

GIFT: FINANCIAL AND MENTAL READINESS CHECKLIST FOR YOU AND YOUR HEIRS

"Any intelligent fool can make things bigger and more complex. It takes a touch of genius and a lot of courage to move in the opposite direction."

—Albert Einstein

INSTRUCTIONS NOT INCLUDED

In a book entitled *Preparing Heirs*, written by Roy Williams and Vick Preisser, a survey was conducted of 3,250 families as to the success or failure of their inheritance. The results proved a 70 percent failure rate and only a 30 percent success rate. Sixty percent of the reason for failure was directly attributed to a breakdown of both communication and trust. Twenty-five percent was due to inadequately prepared heirs. Only 15 percent was noted other with less than 3 percent being poor legal documents, accounting, and finances.

Success, therefore, can be defined as accomplishing just the opposite with open communication, setting proper expectations, and a high degree of trust. With less than 3 percent failure rate attributed to preparing assets, the overwhelming reason for lack of success can be defined as failure to prepare your family.

When so many people fail, you have to pause and learn from others' mistakes. There is a saying known as "rags to riches to rags" that defines this constant cycle of growth of wealth followed by the total loss in the third generation. Similar sayings exist in other countries, so it is important to realize that this is not unique to the US. The reality is that the solutions are very simple, and we make it difficult through inaction.

"People will not do what is in their best interest if it makes them uncomfortable."

—Steve Covey

Action Question: What do you want people to feel, think, and say about you when they hear your name mentioned? How are you signing off on this now?

In an effort to break this cycle and prevent failure for your family, you need to adopt a proven process. It is time to run your own fire drill or dress rehearsal so that you can learn first-hand how your plan will be carried out while you still have time to make impactful improvements.

You can first start by defining *who* you consider family. *What* money, property, resources, and knowledge are you planning to preserve and pass on? *Why* this is important to you, or more specifically, your vision, values, goals, and concerns for the future. Determine *how* you plan on specifically communicating your strategies to improve outcomes. Finally, decide *when* the appropriate timing is to begin this process.

First define for yourself the *who, what, and why* as well as documenting in writing your vision, values, goals, and concerns. These all exist in your current lifestyle, and we will help you think through each. Next, establish *how* you plan to accomplish and communicate your strategies using the tools we will share with you, which are most effectively demonstrated during a family meeting. This will ultimately improve the probability that you will sustain the culture you desire through supporting experiences and family traditions.

Remember, words are easy to say; you are ultimately defined by your actions. In other words, people are more impacted by what you do rather than what you say alone.

DEFINING MOMENTS

Begin to ask yourself and clearly define in writing these four foundational blocks:

- **Vision:** What is your desired future state for you, your wealth and your family? This is when all things align and give life direction and genuine meaning. Amazingly, most people do not have a vision that is clearly defined and written out as they simply have not put life on pause long enough to document one. However, imagine for a moment that you did; what would yours look like?

- **Values**: What are your rules or standards that currently shape your life's decisions? These represent your judgment filters. What is it in your relationships with people and your wealth that you would like to have honored and respected?

- **Goals:** These are small, achievable steps or successes that should be celebrated along the way, which take you closer toward your vision. One needs to define the short-term pains that need to be endured to progress toward the long-term gains. How much are you willing to suffer, sacrifice, or give up to get there? Is your vision grand enough to produce the energy and drive in order to persevere?

- **Concerns:** Very simply, what keeps you up at night? What fears currently exist for your family and your wealth? Remember, fear stands for "false evidence appearing real." You hold the power to "plan" this away!

Action Question: What specific steps are you going to take, guided by your <u>values,</u> that will help you accomplish your <u>goals</u> so that you move away from your <u>concerns</u> and better align your life with your <u>vision</u>?

To prepare for a family meeting, start easy, build interest and momentum as you work toward alignment, and make sure you keep it fun. Consider beginning with your family history with an emphasis on stories about the people and an understanding of how your wealth was created.

It is empowering to understand your past so that you can preserve and appreciate the present and work toward protecting the future for generations to come. A natural family historian is usually born through this process as they capture the stories, organize photos, and memorialize the meaning of your family.

As a means to keep the dream alive and preserve the family history, some governance needs to be established by simply documenting your desired outcomes. These guidelines established need to be realistic for today's society, yet flexible enough to be modified as times change, as things today are very different than they were one hundred years ago. Take as an example our Constitution and the foresight they had to mention or provide permission to rip it up and redo it when it no longer proved appropriate.

Two other areas that are important to define and understand up front is the difference between Financial and Human capital. It is not enough to only focus on the money! A person's financial capital or net worth equals money, property, and resources that can be summed up in a technical term called "stuff."

On the other hand, human capital equates to intellect, skills, knowledge, and the overall condition of well-being or relationships. Long before the time of surplus of stuff, this is all we had to focus on, such as the passing down of skills to perform a trade, or literally survive. We have come a long way.

Action Question: After you convey your stuff, will your family continue to operate as the family unit you desire? Again, are you helping or hurting?

PROGRESSION OF PLANNING

An introduction to our generational wealth planning pyramid provides an easy visual to pull things into perspective. Relationships set the foundation, or really the quality, of those relationships because in the end, this is truly what we seek to preserve. It begins with communication that is open, honest, and transparent. You do not want to leave communication to chance, and it should be verified.

This can be done by setting expectations that are clear, defined, and shared. Remember the only unmet expectation is one that has never been properly communicated. This will all lead to trust that is sincere, reliable, and competent. Nothing else matters if trust does not exist!

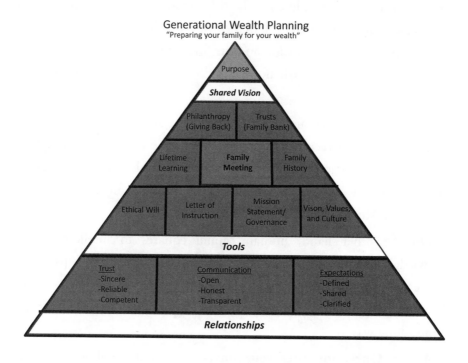

When you think of any quality relationship, these three elements are aligned. Said another way, when a poor relationship exists, typically one or more of these three were violated or damaged. If so, you need to ask if forgiveness is possible to repair the relationship or you cannot move forward.

The building blocks that form the middle of the pyramid are tools providing solutions or strategies that are proven to foster and improve success as you define it. The top of the pyramid results in a shared family vision defining true purpose and equals your personal euphoria when all things exist in balance and harmony.

Consider having each family member create a personalized bucket list of things they want to do or experience during life that supports their purpose, meaning and provides self-fulfillment. Your vision is a clear picture of your future state when alignment is being achieved. Can you think of a better way than working toward achieving your own bucket list and helping those you care deeply about accomplish the same?

Keep in mind that this and several of the tools or strategies are net worth agnostic as several of them do not require one to possess significant sums of money, or money at all, as the focus is on preserving the human capital or family. This will empower them to ultimately become good stewards of your wealth, not just your money.

It is not enough to do your legal documents only and believe that the planning for your wealth transfer is complete. Your legal documents provide you the opportunity to create the framework around how you want your assets ultimately distributed. It is startling that some never even make it to this point and are running around with no documents at all!

The titling of your assets and beneficiary designations need to be properly coordinated to make this a reality, otherwise your documents may not be worth the paper they are printed on. For those who do have proper legal documents and have coordinated all of their holdings appropriately, the often-overlooked next step suggests you color in the framework by communicating your expectations, preferences, and direction through conversations or, preferably, a very simple Letter of Instruction.

If we took ten of our clients' legal documents and laid them side by side and blocked out their names, all of the documents would be very similar if not the same in how they read, especially if you are leaving assets in trust. This is why it is critically important to provide guidance or instructions on how you want to see the assets utilized so that they have the impact you desire and reward your efforts for all of your proactive planning.

Action Question: Why did my parents leave assets in trust? Do they not trust me? This question is often asked by beneficiaries where no communication was provided ahead of time. This reasonable concern gives rise and purpose to why a family meeting and clear communication of expectations coupled with appropriate education needs to occur to prevent a loss in translation.

Imagine for a moment that your parents left you assets in trust and never spoke about their true intentions of leaving assets for you in trust verses outright. Although they were seeking to provide asset protection from potential creditors, divorcing spouses, bankruptcy issues, and possible estate taxes, you may immediately assume they do not trust you or your ability to manage your new wealth.

Now take the case where Mom and Dad had a detailed conversation and provided a written Letter of Instruction regarding the purpose and meaning of why they left assets in trust to protect you and prevent others from getting at your wealth. You have the chance to hear it directly from them and ask questions while they are still here to answer them. This results in an elevation of appreciation and distances you from entitlement with regard to their thoughtfulness, caring, and proactive planning.

You can now begin to internalize the positive impact a simple Letter of Instruction coupled with an open conversation can have on future generations and the resulting appreciation for your efforts it will spawn. This is a non-legal document and costs nothing to produce other than your time. A similar document you can create on your own is an Ethical Will that tends to focus on more of the human capital aspects or values you wish to pass along, life lessons you want remembered, and instills a sense of how you wish to be carried forward.

Lifetime Learning done in an age-appropriate manner allows for continued self-improvement. Its focus can be on formal education, further development of a skilled trade, and promotes the importance of continued personal initiative, drive, and growth.

The role of Philanthropy should be used as a means to teach, give back, serve others, demonstrate caring, and support of causes that are meaningful to you and your family. This can be accomplished with money or donated time, as an abundance of life lessons can be learned in the areas of investing, business acumen, communication skills, socialization, and instilling the importance of being a quality human being, regardless of wealth.

Philanthropy provides an easy way to include younger children and grandchildren in decision-making processes by allowing them to have a voice at the table, do some research, and support causes important to them. The experiences they will gain can be life changing.

Action Question: How would life be different today if you were provided a sum of money that you were required to give away to favorite cause each year? What about sharing an experience of donating your time to a worthy cause as a family unit? What new people would you have met, relationships formed, and awareness generated?

Client Situation: We have clients who have set up private foundations or donor-advised funds with various sums of money and include their children as a means of teaching them an important value of giving back and helping others. The emphasis is not on the money but rather the experience that is being created.

Leaving assets protected in Trust, rather than outright or unprotected, is a preferred method of distribution for those with more significant wealth. It is critically important that the language in the document contain favorable provisions, allowing for maximum flexibility to allow for a positive experience. Hence the importance of working closely with a qualified estate attorney to draft proper documents. After all, they are only going to control EVERYTHING you own!

While the language in the trust documents may be similar, if not exactly the same, for different beneficiaries with different preferences on how they wish to use their funds, the actual application of money can be tailored to that individual's needs.

For example, one child may want to purchase a ski home with their money, and the other one, a beach house. Both can be accommodated. One may want to establish a stock and bond portfolio and another open their own business. With properly drafted documents, each one of these scenarios can be achieved.

Certain Trusts are set up as a Family Bank concept, which is not a product or actual bank, rather simply leaving assets pooled in one account and not disbursed separately. In certain cases, it is easier for specific assets to be bought or preserved for common use such as a block of rental properties or a family business. Money is borrowed from the trust, rather than distributed, at favorable rates and paid back as a means of preserving principal over several generations. Therefore, you could buy your residence or invest in your own business with the trust, providing the capital that ultimately needs to be returned in the form of a loan with interest, no different than a commercial bank.

Collectively the trustees, who are often the children, make the decision on how to invest or loan monies out based upon a formal process that is more relaxed than going to a financial institution. This governance tends to promote responsible decision making and prevent financial mismanagement, as well as reduce the arrogance of entitlement.

Client Situation: We are working with the daughter of a well-to-do couple who has done some advanced planning and has significant wealth that is being left to their four children. However, there has been minimal communication and no instructions on how the wealth should be utilized.

One of the current strategies is causing phantom taxable income with no cash distributions to the four children without warning or explanation, which is proving to be disruptive to the children's personal planning. While Mom and Dad's intentions may be true, their lack of communication and coordination through generations is growing problematic, where good intentions are being tarnished. The solution is simple. They are making it difficult by not communicating directly or through their advisors.

We have developed a Generational Wealth Planning Questionnaire that acts as a conversation starter to help facilitate and promote relationships between family and money as a means to prevent this type of prior situation from occurring.

GIFT: GENERATIONAL WEALTH PLANNING QUESTIONNAIRE

FAMILY MEETINGS

Hosting a family meeting is easier than one might think when you have a process, written agenda, and true purpose that will provide meaning to all who attend. The key is to organize yourself first and solidify your desired outcome for the meeting. You will need to determine ahead of time what information will be shared to promote open discussion and how collective decisions will be made.

You want everybody to know that this is not a therapy session or social gathering. You need to focus on agenda items, provide meaningful impact, and keep it simple while having fun.

"Simplicity is the ultimate sophistication."
—Da Vinci

When do we tell them? The answer to this is early and often, yet it needs to be done in an age-appropriate manner. It can be done directly through formal meetings or one-off conversations. Most do not realize that it is often being done indirectly through observation of your actions, activities, and experiences. And if you do not tell them, the unemotional legal documents one day will with no instructions included!

Hopefully you have coupled them with your own personalized Letter of Instruction, Ethical Will, and maybe even gone so far as to include some family photos and your family history.

What do you tell them? An easy starting point is to review the structure and flow of assets through the documents that you have created. You can openly provide the meaning, intent, thinking, and rationale behind your decisions to leave assets in trust or outright. You have the opportunity to share your vision, your expectations, gain alignment, and earn respect for your efforts.

This can all be accomplished by sharing the details of your net worth or without providing any numbers at all if the timing is not appropriate yet. It is also your choice to decide to include select advisors on your team or just have family around the table. It is often beneficial and helpful in the flow and pace of a meeting to have a facilitator who is not a family member present.

Who should be there? Who is invited will mainly depend upon how you define family and what the topic of conversation being discussed is for the meeting. You can be inclusive of the entire family or exclusive, depending upon the focus. This tends to lead to another question of when does a spouse of a child become family.

To answer this, think through who will be impacted and who the influencers are so that you may control appropriate communication. You can certainly set levels of participation based upon age and appropriateness for the topic. The key to stress here is that it is not all about the numbers but rather about defining expectations and opening up the lines of communication that will facilitate trust and increase the probability of your desired outcome regardless of topics being discussed.

You have to come prepared with a written agenda distributed in advance and no surprises. You definitely want to keep it separate from Thanksgiving dinner and remain focused on the topic at hand. If other worthy causes arise, it may lead to adding that to the agenda depending upon the scope of what was brought up or scheduling another meeting. Everybody should respect the generational differences and come to the meeting open minded and prepared.

When hosting your first family meeting, you may want to start simple, keep it light and have fun with it. An easy topic of discussion is reviewing family history and the source of wealth, coupled with stories attached to each. Another interesting ice breaker that gives everybody an opportunity to participate is to have each person in attendance provide a brief bio of where they are now and where they want to be in the future, as it tends to allow everyone to learn and respect each other's similarities and differences. These are defining personal goals that should be supported and celebrated.

Other topics may include succession of the family business, philanthropy, or intended division of assets, especially when left in unequal portions. The specifics reinforcing decisions may help to prevent family disruption, as everybody has an opportunity to openly discuss the rationale of thinking behind the conclusion.

"When we deal in generalities, we shall never succeed. When we deal in specifics, we shall rarely have a failure. When performance is measured, performance improves. When performance is measured and reported, the rate of performance accelerates."
—Thomas S. Monson

Develop your own personal measurements of success for each meeting. It has been said that you cannot improve what you cannot measure.

Define your starting point, your short-term goals, and long-term vision so you can celebrate progress.

GIFT: SUGGESTIONS FOR A SUCCESSFUL FAMILY MEETING CHECKLIST

Client Situation: A client who found out he was terminally ill wanted to leave behind an extremely important family value dear to him by allowing his daughter to remain at home to raise her child, his first grandchild, and not have to work outside of the home until she was older.

We were able to quantify the resources required to make that a reality, and upon his death only a few months later, money was made available to his daughter and her husband so that she could remain at home for several years to raise their child. This was openly discussed and communicated while he was alive, which led to a successful outcome that was realized and much appreciated by the entire family.

Near the same time frame, another client of similar age died suddenly who had never discussed money with the family. It was considered taboo, and their planning was never fully completed as result. It was upon his death when things turned ugly, as it was discovered that he inadvertently made both his wife and children equal beneficiaries on his life insurance, which was thought to be passing 100 percent to his wife.

One of the children immediately returned the money to Mom because she knew Mom needed it for her own self support. However, the other two refused, keeping the money for themselves, as they felt that was their dad's true intention. And now we will never know. This lack of communication and attention to detail caused a lot of heartache and stressed the remaining family relationships at a time when further emotional complications were tough to handle. This could have been easily avoided.

MEASURING PROGRESS

The way you think and act stems mainly from your deeply rooted beliefs that were shaped by your experiences. Today, it manifests itself in your behaviors that guide your actions. In order to modify actions or behaviors, one needs to alter a belief gained through an experience. *Do what I say, not what I do* is not enough. Children tend to learn more by your actions than they do your words alone.

For example, if you text while driving, yet advise your child who just got their license to never do that, it most likely will never be followed. There is a country song that describes a son in the back seat who uses a bad word when he spilled his drink, and the father asked where he learned to talk like that. The son simply replied, "You, Dad, I want to be just like you" Rodney Atkins, "Watching You."

In the end, it is not just your words but mainly your actions that define who you really are. You will be living the dream when you gain alignment of your entire family's actions that move closer to supporting your purpose. Please realize it will never be perfect, and it is all about continued progress and respect along the path.

You will stand proud knowing that you are moving in the correct direction when family and finance coexist in the same room, around the same conversation in balance and harmony. You will have agreed upon meaning and purpose of both family and money. Further, you will gain accepted responsibilities now and in the future that are evident in the demonstration by each person's actions.

In the end, there will be a significant improvement in the relationship between family and wealth. A simple, five-step process will summarize how you can make this a reality:

- **Unpack:** Literally write out and define your vision, values, goals, and concerns to create a starting point.

- **Debrief:** Begin to communicate where you are and where you would like to be to those who are important, and gain an understanding as well as agreement to continue a fluid and open conversation.

- **Plan**: Determine the tools that you will use to accomplish your short-term goals and move toward your vision. As my friend, Todd Fithian, owner of The Legacy Companies, says, "Tools do not do the job for you; they only make the job easier."

- **Execute:** Put into motion the experiences necessary to shape the beliefs and gain alignment of true, meaningful purpose.

- **Recalibrate:** Since the one constant we will always have is change, embrace it, especially as the wealth cascades down over generations and you protect, preserve, and promote the values that define you as a family.

"Problems cannot be solved by the same level of thinking that created them."
—Albert Einstein

Reach out to your advisory network and make certain that they are performing as a united team and all rowing in the same direction for the benefit of your family. Consider appointing one to be your team captain to help facilitate progress as you continue to coach the entire process along.

Congratulations! You can now visualize how it feels to have prepared your assets for your family coupled with your family being prepared and motivated to accept their responsibilities to become outstanding stewards of your wealth by carrying forward your vision while actively living your values.

Professional Profile:

Craig C. Bartlett, CFP®, CRPC®, CBEC®

Craig.Bartlett@LFG.com | 201-556-4507 |

www.WealthByDesignGroup.com

Craig is the Managing Partner and a Financial Planner at Wealth by Design. In practice since 1995 with the same firm, Craig leverages his years of comprehensive financial-planning experience to further clients' financial well-being and deepen relationships by genuinely helping provide a sense of security.

Craig graduated with honors from the University of Maine earning a Bachelor of Science Degree in Business Administration with a double concentration in Finance and Management. He is a sought-after presenter and has spoken at numerous national conferences, local meetings, and webcasts for Lincoln Financial Advisors (LFA). Craig has also been invited to speak at national industry meetings such as the Financial Planning Association® (FPA®) as well as been interviewed on talk radio station WOR 710.

Craig served for eleven years on LFA's National Planning Conference committee. He is a member of The Resource Group (TRG), which is comprised of LFA's top 200 planners who come together to exchange best practices and improve their planning skills. Craig sits on the TRG Board and heads the Generational Wealth Planning committee and is very active with the Executive Consulting committee. He is also a member in LFA's Sagemark Consulting Private Wealth Services group, which caters to planning for very affluent clients. Craig is a former President on LFA's Premier Partner Advisory Council (PPAC), which is a ten-member committee of planners who collaborate with the top executives of all departments at Lincoln National Corporation. Craig is a longtime member of the Financial Planning Association® (FPA®), the Estate Planning Council of Northern New Jersey (EPCNNJ), and has been a certified sponsor of the New Jersey State Board of Accountancy to teach CPAs their professional continuing education credits.

Craig resides in Morris Township, NJ with his family. He is an active volunteer in the historic Washington Valley Homeowners Association. He supports his alma mater through active donations to a NJ-based scholarship fund and served as a board member of the NJ UMaine Alumni Association. He enjoys volunteering his time for many other rewarding causes such as coaching his daughter's soccer team. Hobbies and interests include travel, fitness, snowmobiling, motorcycle riding, wood working, fishing, raising chickens, and gardening.

CHAPTER SIX

CREATIVE STRATEGIES TO PRESERVE FAMILY WEALTH

By Philip G. Moshier

After close to forty years in this business, working with multiple generations, watching family generations grow, and unfortunately, watching other generations pass away, one of the most significant things that I have learned over the years is that family legacy planning is important. It is the glue that holds the generations together. It helps pass along a legacy to future generations.

Whereas, everyone approaches legacy planning a little differently, when successfully implemented, the end result is the same. I am going to share with you a little of the Moshier family legacy in hopes that you will walk away with a better understanding for my passion as it relates this very important topic.

The first-generation Moshier started in this business in 1926. My grandfather, Leon Moshier, began his career in Akron, Ohio. He worked with a gentleman named Stuart Smith. Stuart Smith was one the legacy founders of the financial advising process.

To this day, *The Creed*, written by Stuart Smith, is distributed to all employees of our firm; the essence of *The Creed*—"Serve First, Last, and Always." My grandfather worked with him for years and carried the same passion and dedication that Stuart Smith did. One of the main businesses he worked with was *The Cleveland Plain Dealer*, which is the daily newspaper in Cleveland.

He worked with many of the employees of the Cleveland PD. Back in those days, the most important way to protect your family long term was through the purchase of insurance. It was the "legacy planning" of the thirties. He touched many families and helped many people through his in-depth knowledge of insurance.

My father, Malcolm Moshier (Mo), came into the business in 1940. He continued to live by the "creed" that Stuart Smith advocated. During his tenure, not only did he continue to help families through the acquisition of Life Insurance but he also helped people plan for their retirement through investments and financial-planning advice.

In 1977, I followed in the footsteps of my father and grandfather and began my career at Connecticut General Life Insurance Company. I worked alongside my father, looking to him for help and guidance while I built my own client base. To this day I still look back and truly appreciate my father being the wonderful mentor and counselor that he was. I believe that his strong support and passion for the business helped me become the quality advisor I am today.

Shortly after I began with Connecticut General, it became CIGNA Financial Advisors. Several years later, the company again transformed, into Lincoln Financial Advisors/Sagemark Consulting. Over the years, I have been able to expand my practice such that I now have a "team" behind me. Using the team approach, we decided to rebrand our name to North Coast Executive Consulting.

After college, I began my career with General Electric Corporation in their financial management program and, shortly after that, their sales management program. After a couple of years, my father asked if I would be interested in a change. In 1977, I left GE and went to work for Connecticut General, and my planning career officially began.

I knew very little about the planning business, but through the help and dedication of my father I began to learn. I told my father I did not want to start in this business working with him and/or working with his clients. I wanted to build my own foundation of clients and advisors. I wanted to make sure that I could succeed in the business—I wanted to make sure that I had the passion necessary for success. I did develop the passion, and it is a passion I still possess to this day.

After several years, we decided to start working together. Our own family legacy issues were arising. My father wanted to slow down in his business, and my grandfather had long since retired. I helped my dad transition into retirement by revisiting their estate plan. This was my first real test with legacy planning. It proved to be a successful process.

One of the last days that my dad was still in the office, I had a very lengthy philosophical discussion with him. He reminded me of *The Creed* and encouraged me to follow that creed with every client that I ever worked with. I still remember him saying, "Phil, serve first, last, and always, and the rest of life will take care of itself."

That is something that truly resonated with me over the years. I have met dozens and dozens of wonderful people who have become my clients. I have offered quality guidance to my clients and their families over the years and have seen many of them retire, become grandparents, and even a few of them are great-grandparents.

All of this could not be done without the incredible team that I have in place. My team shares the same passion as I do, and we pride ourselves on superior client service. Whereas I currently do not have a fourth-generation Moshier in the wings waiting to carry on the family legacy, I am confident that the team that I have in place will take care of our clients/families for decades to come.

EDUCATIONAL LEGACY

When I look back at the legacy planning that my father did, the one thing that I can certainly relate to was his Educational Legacy Planning. My dad attended Denison University. He met my mom at Denison, and they were married in 1940. I attended Denison University as well, and that is where I met my wife. We were married in 1975. My daughter also attended Denison.

I guess you could say we have a sort of "family legacy" at Denison. My dad was an avid supporter of Denison University; he helped build the SAE, or the Sigma Alpha Epsilon, Fraternity House there. He and my mother were also very involved on campus and in the Denison community. When Dad passed away in 2000, in addition to all the money he had donated to the college over his working years, he left a generous gift that was invested into an education endowment for the purpose of financially assisting students.

Every year, five students receive a very nice scholarship to help them pay for their education. My parents' passion for education was something that was very important to them, and therefore to me as well. Over the years I have advised many clients on this topic as well.

Certainly something else I learned early on was that a client and/or a family is best served with a team approach of professional collaboration. This collaboration can be with an attorney and/or a CPA. This is critical for the benefit of the client because it is the collective wisdom of this team of professionals that always harnessed creative planning ideas in the ever-increasingly complex world we all live.

Whereas Educational Legacy is certainly important, it is certainly at the discretion and wishes of the client. Educational Legacy is not something that would "make or break" the client and the legacy that they wish to pass on. Charitable giving is certainly a topic that needs to be discussed, but I feel that that next couple of topics that I cover are truly the nuts and bolts of Legacy Planning.

PRESERVATION OF A BUSINESS

The next topic that I am going cover is a family in which there were three generations of an operating steel company. My father began working with the grandfather in the mid-fifties. My dad was assigned to their group life insurance program. Dad rewrote the plan, was able to increase coverage for all the employees, and actually saved the company money.

The grandfather appreciated the effort that my dad took to take care of the business and employees. Let me say as a side note, it wasn't easy, as over the years the grandfather had a bias against life insurance and certainly any business planning.   In spite of the pushback that he received from the grandfather, my dad had also put a retirement plan in place for the business so he had a strong foundation with the two older generations. As it turned out, my father and the second generation of the business were college friends and were in the same fraternity.

I first met the third generation in 1980. I remember discussing business succession planning in order to help preserve the business for future generations. The grandfather felt he did not need to listen to us because he had "the grand plan." As several of the shareholders passed away from this wonderful family business, the company was required to purchase/redeem their shares of stock for cash.

The company did not have the necessary liquidity available to do this and therefore had to borrow money from the bank to buy the stock back. This became very costly over the years.

The steel business in the early eighties was very depressed. In addition to the steel business being depressed, they had opened up two new distribution locations and incurred a significant amount of additional bank debt. The banker was getting very nervous, so we discussed the idea of key man life insurance on the father, or the second generation. Key man life insurance involves the business securing a life insurance policy on a key employee in an amount of a calculated loss the business may incur if that key employee dies. The business is the owner, premium payor, and beneficiary of that policy, with the key employee being the insured.

Even though the father was not in perfect health, he thought it would be a good idea. That is when the two younger owners understood the need to protect the business for all the employees and future family generations working in the business.

My dad was very passionate in his recommendation of making sure that the company procured key man insurance. After much persuasion, they did get key man insurance in place. Even though the grandfather's attitude was quite negative about the idea, he knew that it was the right thing to do. My dad had a way of encouraging clients to move forward, and he had that unconditional commitment to serve and to take care of his clients. I used to call this the *"care factor."*

He had that ingredient that is so hard to come by in our competitive business. He took the time to understand his clients and their families, understand their concerns, and appeal to their interests. More than anything, he wanted to grow with them and learn from them.

That is another one of the important lessons I learned early in my career, that the desire to serve must be so sincere and so honest that our clients not only feel it initially but continue to feel it throughout our long-term relationship with them.

As I said, this particular steel company owed the bank about two million dollars. The business climate was not the strongest at the time, and the loan officer wanted to drop the company from the bank's books and they wanted to call the loan. We did finally secure life insurance on the father. As it turned out, the father ended up passing away a few years later, and the money came into the business to pay off the majority of the bank debt.

When the large sum of money was delivered to the business, we had created tax-free dollars. The plan that we had put in place to help sustain the business long term had worked. The bottom line was that the majority of the bank debt was payed off and now the grandson owned a business almost debt free.

Fortunately the life insurance proceeds took the pressure off all the officers of the company, and it gave all of them the time they needed to better master the business and put them on a better and sound financial basis.

When we delivered those dollars and the family kept the business solvent, they had over forty employees that remained employed. We were able keep a roof over their heads and food on their tables and keep their retirement dreams alive. Not only had we helped to develop the plan that created the capital for the second generation, but the business successfully transferred to the third generation.

It was the ultimate feeling of success—when you realize all the planning really worked and everything that my dad and I said would happen did happen. I remember sitting with another one of my dad's friends way back when, and he said that we are the heartbeat of financial advising. We are the key to whether or not a client has done those things he or she must do. Whereas other advisors are certainly important, other advisors deliver bills, we, all of us on the planning side, create and deliver dollars.

When the father died, I helped the widow. When the older officers retired, I remember helping each and every one of them plan their exit from the business. We made sure that they had proper legal documents, we rolled over their retirement plans into IRAs, we helped them consolidate various investment accounts, and we made sure that they secured nursing home care or insurance for those who wanted it.

We also set up systematic withdrawal programs for them to make sure that they received the money that they needed to live on day-to-day. When they reached age 70½, we set up their required minimum distributions on a year in and year out basis.

Something again that I learned from this life experience with my father is that work does not stop when a particular sale is made; it begins a life commitment to our clients. It gave me so much pride that all the retirees of this particular business wanted to work with me and my team. As Dad had repeated over the years, if you take care of the clients and serve them first, last, and always, over the long run the business will take care of itself.

I truly believe that building long-term relationships with my clients is one of the keys to my successful business career.

FAMILY LEGACY

This family legacy scenario began with a senior corporate executive of a very large public company. I began working with the senior executive a little over twenty-five years ago, just before he retired. He was the VP of Finance. He was extremely interested in retirement planning, ideas for retirement planning, and how to plan going forward.

I remember when I met with him for the first time. I explained our comprehensive planning services and explained that in order to have these services we would be charging a fee. I helped him see the value in planning and the value associated with the planning fee.

He understood that it was important to engage us, because of the expertise we could offer, and pay that planning fee, for good-quality advice was an important part of retirement planning. We compiled a significant amount of financial, legal, and tax information and had many meetings with him and his wife to understand their goals, objectives, and retirement dreams.

He certainly knew the day-to-day business and financials of the multi-billion dollar company, but he had never fully understood his *individual* financials. In other words, how everything that he had worked a lifetime to accumulate would help him live more comfortably in retirement and hopefully have a legacy to pass to future generations.

We were able do an analysis on when to take Social Security, whether we file early, delay filing, or file late in order to leverage benefits. We were able to look at his investment accounts and figure out the most tax-efficient way to take income. We were able to look at the entire picture and fit all of the pieces together.

Someone had to take the lead to assess all this information in order to prepare a comprehensive analysis. The client wanted to be educated as to all of the potential options to solve their various issues, and each one certainly had a cost/benefit associated with it. In order to facilitate the plan with the family, all the advisors had to meet periodically and review the various options. This allowed them to have a general consensus of the implementation strategies.

We all had one common purpose, to do what is in the best interest of the family. I remember when we analyzed the defined benefit pension and whether we should take a monthly income or roll it over. We looked at the 401(k), and since there was corporate stock in it, we were able to do a NUA (Net Unrealized Appreciation).

I did a comprehensive investment analysis of everything that they owned and had accumulated over the years. They really did not know why they owned and/or how it fit in to the overall investment portfolio strategy. Because of the comprehensive planning and strategizing that we implemented, we continued to earn his confidence and trust over the years.

I have worked with this client since 1990, and he is now in his eighties. The trust that we have generated over the years has now allowed me the opportunity to do generational planning. I am working with his children and even a few of his grandchildren.

We have helped educate the family about unique gifting strategies. My client has been encouraged to take advantage of these strategies, and we have been implementing them over the years in order to keep dollars out of the hands of the IRS.

The Estate planning strategies continued to be implemented over the years. However, this client had another issue to deal with—a concentrated stock position. This required a lot of creative planning on our part. Early on, we discussed the estate tax exemptions, the top marginal tax brackets, and as the estate exemptions grew from a mere $600,000 in the early 2000s, there was a lot of exposure to the IRS. Even though the exemption has increased over the years to over $5,000,000 through 2017 and, under the current administration, over $11,000,000, there is still exposure because of the size of the estate. However, over the years we were able to implement several creative strategies to help preserve the family wealth.

Early on in our planning process we purchased a second-to-die policy that was taken out in 1994 when the estate exemption was very low. At that point there was $1.7 million of death benefit with an annual premium of $37,000. Because the estate tax brackets had grown and increased over the years, we discussed the purchase of an additional second-to-die policy. I worked with our home office insurance team, and we came up with a very creative strategy for the second policy.

Our strategy had to do with leveraging his concentrated corporate stock position. We decided it would be a good idea to gift stock under the unique estate exemption and annual gifting limitations. We gifted $1 million worth of stock, and at age seventy-three and seventy-four we were able to leverage it up and secured $3,500,000 worth of life insurance in an irrevocable life insurance trust (ILIT).

The strategy was simple; we gifted $1 million of corporate stock, and the dividends were paid to the ILIT. The potential growth of the stock and dividends would be enough to pay ten years of premiums. The result—$3,500,000 of tax-free life insurance guaranteed. The one factor that really worked in our favor was the significant capital appreciation of the gifted stock.

So, in summary, seven years ago we put in $1 million worth of stock, we have payed $110,000 premium per year for seven years ($770,000 of total premium dollars), and there is still $800,000 of stock in the trust. Where we thought the $1 million was going to be leveraged to deliver the

$3,500,000 of second-to-die life insurance, in fact the $3,500,000 life insurance policy is almost paid up and there is still $800,000 worth of corporate stock in this ILIT. The amount of tax-free dollars for the family is actually $4,300,000.

Whereas it is certainly important to secure life insurance in order to preserve your estate, it is equally as important to consider Long-Term Care Insurance. This was another area that I was able to add value. I was able to introduce a unique long-term care product that uses a linked benefit that provides access to a combination of cash value, death benefit, and long-term care benefit.

Instead of paying an annual premium, the client was able to put $100,000 into one of these linked benefit policies. This policy gave them significant long-term care benefits for home health care, assisted living, nursing home, and Alzheimer's care, as well as a number of other assisted living services. Additionally, if the money that they put into the policy was not used for any long-term care need, there was an ultimate death benefit that was substantially greater than the lump sum deposit they initially put into it. Plus, if they wanted to terminate the policy during life, a refund of 80-100 percent of premium is available based upon design. Again, a very unique product for those who can afford to self-insure yet want to transfer some risk.

In addition to preserving a legacy for his family, church and community were also extremely important. They also had several other charities that they were very involved with. After many discussions with the attorney and the CPA, it was decided to establish a family foundation.

They gifted another significant block of low-basis corporate stock to the family foundation. They would be able to use the mandatory annual distributions established by the IRS from the family foundation to accommodate their annual gifting wishes to various charities. More importantly, they could involve all four children in the annual distribution decisions.

Establishing the family foundation is now something that all four children are involved in, and the mother and father's wishes to be charitably inclined will be carried forward for many years to come. The children get to decide what charities they would like to have a portion of the annual distributions go to, which makes the parents extremely happy.

The bottom line on working with this family for over twenty-five years is that we have implemented several planning strategies for the family, children, and grandchildren. It gives our team tremendous satisfaction knowing the comprehensive job we have done, especially in working with three generations.

I remember talking with the father at one point, and he said to me, "You do love your children equally, but we must treat them all uniquely." This resonated with me, and I always remember it as I work with other clients and help them with their legacy planning.

THE WIDOW

This was another couple I was introduced to from another happy client. It was interesting, when I met them in 2004 they both worked for the same company. One was an engineer and one was the director of HR. It was a very unique situation because it was a second marriage for both, so we were pulling together a lot of personal data, documents, cash flow summaries, and tax returns for two different families.

Since they were recently married, it was something that was important for them because they wanted to understand if they had the flexibility to retire in the very near future and how to combine or separate assets among the various family members.

In gathering all this personal information, sitting down with them and having lengthy discussions as far as what their goals and objectives were, we also needed to develop a stock option exit strategy as well as retirement cash flow modeling. These lengthy discussions also involved investment risk tolerances. We were very thorough in understanding what their risk tolerance was by going through a series of questions.

Since they had pensions and 401(k) plans to roll over, we went through and educated them on various portfolio opportunities in order to help them achieve their lifestyle cash flow requirements. We also discussed with them how important it would be to have a long-term relationship with an advisor who would effectively monitor these portfolios and make the appropriate changes with the ebb and flow of the investment world.

Because there were two sets of children, the planning in general became very tricky, and there were many interesting discussions with the estate attorney to determine what kind of estate documents would be appropriate for them, especially since they were soon to become proud grandparents.

We needed to understand the ownership of all their assets, their homes, and their investment accounts so that we could understand how to best accommodate their goals and objectives.

After understanding what was important to them, we had numerous educational discussions and offered them different solutions that would reduce and/or minimize Federal transfer expenses and/or Ohio inheritance taxes. On the estate planning side I remember when we collaborated with the estate attorney to be sure the proper legal documents were drafted in order to accommodate the unique extended family circumstances. We also saw the need for an irrevocable life insurance trust (ILIT).

Shortly after retirement the husband had a series of illnesses. He passed away in December of 2013. The life insurance that he owned went into a trust for the wife's lifetime benefit. When his trust became flush with cash at the husband's passing, we explored the opportunity to secure long-term care insurance on the surviving wife.

I introduced a unique long-term care product that was reviewed with the widow and the children. The children were in agreement with our planning ideas. I have always found it is extremely important to have agreement by all parties so everyone is on the same page.

Not only did it again cover multiple long-term care situations but it also had a death benefit, so if the long-term care benefits were never used they would recover 100 percent plus of the cash that was put toward this policy. The children thought it was a very creative use for some of the funds in the father's trust.

Because of the strong and trusted relationship that I had with the couple, the children asked us for guidance after they received their inheritance from their father. We are privileged to be working with another generation of a family.

The good news is that their accumulated net worth and life insurance proceeds provided the widow with ample assets to sustain her lifestyle throughout her lifetime. The widow's concern was preservation of the wealth for their children and grandchildren. She was insurable and decided to purchase a single life insurance policy with an annual gift of $27,000 a year for $2.5 million of tax-free death benefit for the children and grandchildren.

This death benefit will provide substantial income-tax-free dollars to the children and/or grandchildren so that during her lifetime she is not concerned if she uses up all her assets, whether it is with traveling or gifting to the family or going on family vacations, knowing that the kids will receive an inheritance down the road when she passes away.

In wrapping up this short chapter you can see there are several themes that run true for these three family situations. One was preservation of a business, one was family legacy and having adequate liquidity, and the last was making sure the widow would not have a care in the world for herself being a widow and that the children would ultimately have an inheritance no matter what happened to the mom.

When you add it all up and look at different strategies to preserve family wealth or to preserve life for your children and grandchildren, there are different approaches and multiple solutions. I pride myself in offering different solutions and educating our clients to the different solutions and what the financial and tax impact might or could be in making a decision.

Every client before he or she makes a decision is well informed and certainly makes an educated decision on what will be best for them and their families, both short term and long term.

In summary, in specializing with working with the affluent families that we have been blessed to work with over the years and establishing harmony among the family members and understanding the family vision and values, I know that all is okay for our clients, all is okay for their families, and all is okay for those who want to take care of their community.

Professional Profile:
Philip G. Moshier, CFP°, CRPC°, AEP°

Philip.Moshier@NorthCoastExecutive.com | 216-591-2350 |
www.NorthCoastExecutive.com

Phil is the Managing Partner and President of North Coast Executive Consulting. Phil has consistently achieved Lincoln Financial Advisors Corporation highest performance awards and top industry recognition for outstanding performance and quality service for his clients. Phil represents the third generation of Moshiers serving the financial needs of clients. He is a lifetime member of The Resource Group, a group which consists of the top 200 planners in the company. Lincoln Financial Advisors has consistently recognized him as being in the leading 1 percent of Advisors in the country. Phil has been honored form 2013 to 2016 by Lincoln Financial Advisors by receiving the regional "Planner of the Year" award for his region. This award recognizes excellence in the financial-planning field.

Phil's approach for financial planning sets him apart from others in the industry since his analysis and recommendations encompass all aspects of an individual's situation—including estate tax strategies, retirement-planning opportunities, employee-stock-options strategies, and legacy planning. His work consistently demonstrates his unique ability to deliver creative solutions to his clients' complex financial concerns. He believes in establishing long-term relationships with his clients, and his services entail the design, implementation, and constant review of the financial plan in order to remain consistent with the clients' every changing needs and tax law changes.

Phil is a graduate of Denison University with a bachelor's degree in Economics. Phil also holds an advanced degree in the areas of Investment Strategy and Portfolio Management.

He has been involved in many charitable organizations and is currently a board member for the Crohn's & Colitis Foundation. For the past twenty years, Phil has co-chaired the Annual Golf Tournament which has raised a total of $2,500,000 under his leadership. He was the past President of the Cleveland Estate Planning Council. Chairman of the Board of The Resource Group (2018–2019).

Phil is a longtime Cleveland resident and currently resides in Pepper Pike. His hobbies include golf, watching sporting events, and enjoying time with his three grandchildren in Denver.

CHAPTER SEVEN

CONSIDERATIONS FOR A BUSINESS OWNER

By Michael McFeeley

There are many more complexities that business owners have in their financial lives than the average person. Coordinating their business and personal planning is a key element to success in your overall financial planning. For most business owners, and individuals for that matter, if you had to line up all your advisors in one room, they would most likely be meeting for the first time.

Many business owners have business attorneys to draft business documents and personal attorneys who will do their estate documents. Also, they will have investment advisors or pay roll companies that will give them advice on their business plans and others for their personal investments.

For most business owners their greatest asset is the value of their business, and it is usually the reason they have been so well compensated throughout their financial lives. With that taken into consideration we should assess our business as an asset, and it should be taken into consideration with your personal assets, objectives, and goals to help you reach financial independence. We need to understand the risk we are taking with our business, the returns that we are making, and most importantly, the cash flow that it is creating just like any other asset we would assess. The question becomes, "Are we being compensated for the risk we are taking? Are we being as tax efficient as possible?"

For business owners, we want to look at your situation from a cross-disciplinary basis, not just a legal, accounting, or financial perspective, but across the board. By doing this you are able to identify planning gaps and opportunities that you can insert and be better compensated for the risk, be more tax efficient and at the end of the day, be able to put more dollars in your pocket.

Commonly we find that accountants that are either personal or business accountants most do not know the advanced investment solutions to bring to the table, as it is not their primary business, so we end up paying more in taxes than we should. This is certainly not in all cases, but we commonly find a disconnect between advisors and accountants.

Investment advisors are usually brokers that will pick investments, whether it is mutual funds, stocks, or even help you set up a 401(k) or retirement plan; however, they are usually picking investments. By looking at things from a cross-disciplinary basis, maybe the investment advisor can present investment ideas that will help reduce your tax burden and that will be a better fit depending on your situation. There are opportunities to create passive losses/gains, active losses, or even tax-free or tax-advantaged growth.

From a legal perspective, you also should have your legal documents reviewed and coordinated to make sure ownership of your company matches up with your estate documents. For example, who is going to make the tough decisions when something happens to you or your partner due to death, disability, or even deadlock in the case of equal ownership? Coordinating your personal documents with your business documents is very important in that doom or gloom scenario.

Finally, you want to look at your overall insurance portfolio to make sure you are covered on all fronts from property/casualty, liability, life, health, disability, and even long-term care. Many business owners have accumulated enough or are on the right track to gain financial independence, and we believe that success is worth protecting. In this day and age, anybody can be sued for anything. In the Liebeck v. McDonald's restaurant case, Stella Liebeck was awarded $2.68 million dollars for spilling "defective" hot coffee on her lap. Fortunately, McDonald's can handle a lawsuit such as this but not every business owner can.

These reasons are why it is important to have one advisor or team who plays quarterback and looks at your situation from a cross-disciplinary basis. This advisor should serve as a think tank for your team of advisors and other advisors who bring their best and brightest ideas to help accomplish your goals. Finally, they have to be your advocate in the marketplace.

The lack of coordination for most can mean hundreds of thousands, if not millions, of dollars, depending on the situation. One good example of a lack of coordination is a client that has a $45 million dollar business. They have $2 million of investible assets, and because of current estate tax laws, their attorneys brought a great idea to the table.

That idea was to gift at a large discount, roughly 60 percent of his business for estate tax purposes into a family trust for his children. That would be great planning, except neither the financial advisors, accountants, or attorneys that were working with the client ever really understood the cash flow needed in retirement to maintain this client's needs.

So with this client having roughly $2 million of investable assets and spending close to $750,000 per year, the remaining assets that were not in trust, even once liquidated and taxes were paid, could not cover the expenses and could not let him maintain the lifestyle he was trying to live in retirement. That is fantastic estate planning from the attorneys in order to reduce future estate taxes; the problem is they put the cart before the horse and did not assess the situation from a holistic view.

Many people have written entire books on considerations that business owners should take in their business, so one chapter is only going to cover the tip of the iceberg. This is going to be a mile-high review of common pitfalls or opportunities we see for business owners.

Certainly you should consult an advisor, an attorney, or an accountant on any of the ideas that may or may not make sense to figure out how they work in your independent situation. My goal for this chapter is to show the business owner a few creative design ideas, explain why you need an advocate in the marketplace, and illustrate why an advisor who addresses your situation on a cross-disciplinary basis will best serve you.

CASH FLOW AND BUDGET

Those seem to be simple terms that everybody should understand, whether you are a business owner or not. The problem is when you dive down deep, cash flow and budget drive any financial planning, whether it is how much we can put away on an annual basis and how much we are spending or how much we need to accumulate over the course of our lives to be able to retire and maintain our lifestyle.

Once again, the reoccurring theme throughout this chapter is, you need to understand the business and the personal aspects of your cash flow. Far too often do clients and advisors assume the successful business owner is going to be okay. "I have a valuable asset, I make a lot of money, and it is always going to be this good." We always say winners keep score, and once we have gathered enough assets that you, your family, and your legacy are going to be financially independent, then maybe you win.

Commonly, we meet the $35 million business owner who makes $2 million a year, we walk in and think, *They have lots of planning gaps but they will be fine.* When completing a cash flow analysis, realize that spending $3 million a year will not be maintained with the succession of the business and that they are going to run out of money in their seventies, or forced to take risks in investments that would not be prudent, or spend less.

I would like to touch on a few strategies that business owners use to reduce their annual tax burden, which will allow them to invest more into the business and more money in their pockets.

BUSINESS STRUCTURE

There are many ways that we can structure our business and some that will improve cash flow. Most of the corporate structures that are utilized are an LLC, or Limited Liability Company, an LLP, which is a Limited Liability Partnership, or to incorporate, which most business owners will do to add a layer of asset protection to their business and isolate it from their personal assets. On a sole proprietorship or partnership, one may have asset-protection issues and liability that may flow to your personal assets. We also will explore the pros and cons of a corporation, C Corporation, and a Sub-Chapter S Corporation.

First, which is by far the most common business that we see, is a company that is an LLC. An LLC has the ability to file as a sole proprietor, partnership, and Sub-Chapter S Corporation. These are all pass-through entities with pros and cons but the most tax advantaged under current tax law is the S Corporation.

There are some cons to an S Corporation. An S-Corp is limited to one hundred shareholders. When we take distributions verses salary and bonuses, they have to be done proportionately based on ownership, which may or may not be a good thing. There are more requirements, such as annual meetings and some documentation to show we are doing the things a corporation should do versus a sole proprietor that uses their business account as just another bank account or asset that they can do whatever they wish with.

One of the most attractive reasons people will choose a Sub-Chapter S Corporation is because of distributions that they can take once they have hit a reasonable salary for their profession. What does that exactly mean?

When we take a salary and we are an employee of a company, or even an employer, and we act as a sole proprietor, we have to pay federal income taxes, state taxes, Social Security, and Medicare taxes as the employer, which is combined 7.65 percent, and the employee, which is a combined 7.65 percent. As a sole proprietor you pay 15.3 percent on your earnings up to Social Security limits, and once you have met your Social Security max, it then drops down to just the Medicare limits, which are currently 2.9 percent.

The advantage of an S Corporation is that the business owner that makes $250,000 can take $125,000 salary and $125,000 in a distribution and he will save roughly 3 percent on that $125,000. In some states it may be greater because you can avoid local taxes and city taxes. You need to check with your accountant and see how it would benefit you in your current situation. A more powerful situation people would choose an S Corporation is for the business owner who makes $100,000 and is a one-man shop. If the reasonable salary for the type of work that this person does is $50,000 and they take a $50,000 salary, they will pay federal taxes, state taxes, Social Security, and Medicare taxes as an employer and an employee.

The remaining $50,000 will be taken as a distribution and avoid 15.3 percent in taxes, which is over $7,500 to that person, and that is a big deal from an income and tax efficiency perspective. One of the impacts that has to be taken into account when reducing your salary is what type of retirement plan you will choose.

The retirement plan is based off of salaries and bonuses, not distributions. Let's use the example I just gave with the $100,000 of income that the individual made and was taking $100,000 in salary and paying all the associated taxes. We commonly see utilization of a

SEP IRA, or a Simplified Employee Pension. With a SEP you are able to put away 25 percent of your income, which would have been roughly $25,000, into a retirement account that would be tax deferred assuming all $100,000 was taken as salary.

From a business standpoint we look and say, "What else could we do?" What is commonly missed is that one would be able to utilize a solo 401(k) as opposed to the SEP IRA if they are the only employee of the company or husband and wife. A solo (k) allows one to put away $19,000 per year (2019 limit) as long as we have a $19,000 salary and are under the age of fifty; an additional $6,000 catch-up contribution (2019 limit) if age of fifty that year or older.

In this scenario we are able to put away $25,000 in a solo 401(k), plus the ability to do profit sharing, which is an additional 25 percent of his salary. In this case we are able to reduce our income to $50,000 and take distributions of $50,000 and still be able to put away more money in a tax-deferred retirement plan by structuring the correct type of plan.

That is one high level story of the advantages of an S Corporation. There are also disadvantages, as I mentioned, with flexibility and how people are compensated when you have multiple partners and if those partners have different compensation levels, but there are ways to work through these hurdles and still be tax efficient.

The final type of tax structure would be the C Corporation. The C Corporation has many advantages, and it also has many disadvantages. This type of corporation has the potential of being the least favorable tax scenario because of double taxation, and that is the reason that most small business owners do not choose the C Corporation.

An example of double taxation would be if you have $1 million in the bank, the corporation will pay roughly 50 percent of taxes (hypothetical tax bracket), and then when you distribute it to yourself, you have to pay your federal and state tax rate.

———

One million dollars turns into roughly $250,000 in the pocket of that business owner when they are at the highest tax bracket, including state taxes. An S Corporation, partnership, or sole proprietor will pass through and the $1 million will be roughly $500,000 without doing other tax planning in a 50 percent state and federal bracket.

Double taxation is the biggest downside of the C Corporation. There is no great way to get money out of the business tax preferred besides utilizing certain types of retirement plans and employee benefits, and then there are some advantages of the C Corporation for those things. However, they have to be explored and cash flow has to be very good for them to work.

The C Corporation along with its many formalities is typically used because it has the ability to have many owners and different share classes of stocks or stockholders. Companies that are trying to raise money or want to go public on the exchange are typically C Corporations because you can have as many shareholders as you would like and you can have different classes of stock, whether it be voting, non-voting, A shares, B shares, preferred stock, and common stock; there are many different types of ownership.

When choosing a C Corporation, you have to really understand the benefits of why you need to be a C Corporation and understand the benefits that come along with this type of corporation to see if it is efficient from a tax standpoint.

One final pitfall we see with business owners is that many times the business owner will own their real estate or property as well as owning the business in the same corporation, LLC, or even personally. You should consider having the real estate, if possible, owned in a separate entity or titled to where you are protecting your personal assets or the business assets that utilize the real estate. If someone is skateboarding on your property and gets injured, you do not want them to be able to come after the business or your personal assets.

The advantage of owning your own real estate is certainly not paying rent and building an asset. There is also a tax advantage when you pay yourself rent and you take out those rental dollars. Those dollars typically do not have to pay Social Security and Medicare taxes. Remember to consult with your tax professional, as they can help with the particulars of your situation.

REDUCING TAXES WITH EMPLOYER PLANS

The next way that I am going to highlight reducing or deferring taxes is employer plans. There are many different types of employer retirement plans, and it depends on the structure of your company, the number of employees, demographic of the employees, and the amount of income you are looking to shelter.

I will start with some of the more common plans that we see. I mentioned for the sole proprietor or the individual business owner that an SEP is a common retirement plan that we see, which means that you can put away up to 25 percent of your income each year.

The problem with this type of plan is that if you do add employees, it becomes very costly, as you are required to put away roughly the same percentage for those employees as you do yourself without any employee contribution. An SEP is typically not the ideal plan unless you are looking to retain key employees or are looking to make generous contributions for your employees, which is fantastic if that is your goal as the business owner. If your goal is to put away as much for you and still make sure you can attract and retain employees with an employer plan or a retirement plan, then you should consider other strategies.

The next plan that we commonly see is a Simple IRA. The Simple IRA allows you to put away $13,000 (2019 limit) if you are under the age of fifty and an additional $3,000 catch-up contribution (2019 limit) if you are age of fifty or older that year. With the Simple plan, any of your employees who contribute 3 percent, you have to contribute 3 percent in a match for them.

There are some rules with the Simple IRA if you cannot make the match and the corporation is struggling to avoid the event, but it should be consistent. Typically you are matching 3 percent for yourself and your employees, but that only gives you a certain level of tax-deferred savings. The simple IRA is a low-cost plan that does not need to be administered, and sometimes that is the right option if your deferral is within the range allowed.

The most common type of plan we see in the business-owner market is the 401(k). The 401(k) has many different layers for planning. The first layer is the employee contribution of $19,000 up to age fifty and $6,000 catch-up contribution age fifty and beyond. The problems for business owners are the funding requirements and testing. ERISA looks at the contributions of all employees, and it could limit the business owners' contributions as it is tested so the Highly Compensated employees are not the only benefactors.

This is why most popular 401(k) plans are Safe Harbor Plans. There are two different types of Safe Harbor Plans that will allow the business owner to contribute the maximum amount of dollars. These are the minimum requirements. The first is a 3 percent flat contribution that the employer puts in for everybody, no matter what happens or how much they defer.

The second is a Safe Harbor match, which is dollar for dollar on the first 3 percent and then 50 cents for the next 2 percent. If an employee contributes 5 percent, they will get the maximum match, but that is only to the employees who are contributing to their plan. Under both circumstances the highly compensated are then allowed to defer the maximum amount of dollars.

The next plan in addition to a 401(k) is a Profit Sharing Plan. The Profit Sharing Plan is really layered on top of the 401(k), but it allows the business owner to put away $56,000 (2019 limit) in one year or $62,000 if age of fifty plus. Some businesses have determined it makes more sense to utilize a Profit Sharing plan on its own without a 401(k), which can be done. The profit sharing is also cross tested against all your other employees, and so you will have to contribute a portion of the employees' salaries so that you can defer the maximum. Depending on the type of company you have, that might be very favorable, or it might not really be an option because of the amount of dollars that it is going to cost you.

Looking at your company, breaking down the types of employees you have, and sectoring out who the highly compensateds are and are not may help you put more dollars away or build a better plan that allows you to put more away tax deferred. The profit sharing has to be looked at very carefully and analyzed with your company and employees to see how valuable this plan is for you.

The final type of plan for the small business owner is the plan that when I tell people they ask, "Why have my advisors never discussed this with me?" Many advisors will talk about 401(k) and even Profit Sharing Plans, but to add on a Defined Benefit or Cash Balance Plan gives the business owner the ability to put significantly more dollars away per year.

This type of plan is determined by having a lump sum value at age sixty-five, which in 2019 is approximately $2.6 million. Recently we established a plan with a business owner who is age fifty-five and was allowed to contribute an additional $100,000 per year into that plan. Frankly, he could have contributed more if that was the goal. Cash Balance plans can be a very powerful tool to reduce your tax burden but, like any investment, it does have some liability and should be further analyzed.

With any retirement plans, we need to take into account the employees, the risk, and the advantages and disadvantages of each. It is also very important to understand the cash flow of the business and how much that you would like to save, defer taxes, and reduce your tax burden.

One final story to wrap up the retirement planning section and the ways to reduce taxes through understanding your cash flow and budget is a story of two business owners that had four employees who were making about $750,000 each. They were in their mid-fifties, and their goal was to put away as much as possible. When we met them they were utilizing a 401(k) and a Profit Sharing Plan and putting away approximately $59,000 a year. Great, but not going to get them to where they needed to be for retirement because of their tax brackets and spending, for that matter.

We were able to utilize a Cash Balance Plan that actually did not include some of their employees and allowed each of them to put away an additional $150,000 to $180,000 per year into a retirement plan, but that is not all. We were also able to utilize insurance inside of the retirement plan, which meant they were able to put away more dollars than the average Defined Benefit Plan because of the way insurance is structured inside the Defined Benefit Plan. This is an advanced strategy and has to be understood by the owner but can make a lot of sense in certain scenarios.

At the end of the day, winners keep score and business owners need to understand their cash flow. It is paramount to their financial independence. There are many opportunities, and this was the tip of the iceberg.

LEGAL DOCUMENTS

Now that we understand our cash flow and how we structure our company, we need to understand what legal documents we should have as a business owner. Many documents that we see from business owners are legal but not viable. Documents will have provisions in a buy/sell agreement, for example, with two partners, which states that thirty days after that partner has deceased, the remaining business owner must pay in full to that person's spouse, estate, or family. Then when we ask the business owner, "How do you feel about coming up with $5 million in thirty days?" and they say, "That is not possible," which means they have a legal document but it is not a viable document.

We are going to go through some of the legal documents that business owners should have and some of the common pitfalls that we see that make these legal documents not viable. We have legal documents to protect us during doom-or-gloom situations but also to set expectations and valuations for our company.

Once again, the theme of this chapter is to coordinate your personal planning with your legal planning. It is common that a business owner owns their business in their own name, as opposed to potentially owning that business in an LLC or revocable trust, which could avoid probate costs, delays, publicity upon passing.

How much is your business worth six months after you are gone? The ability to sell assets immediately can be very important. I have dealt with business owners who have only been able to sell their files after passing away for $25,000 when their business was worth $400,000 to $600,000.

The typical documents that are needed are the corporate organizational documents and sometimes a standalone buy/sell agreement to address the issues that partners face. Below are some of the big issues that should be addressed.

Valuation—Discussing how we value our business in these documents is a very important piece especially in the doom-or-gloom scenario. Most documents have formulas, but formulas can be manipulated. Some have appraisal methodology, which is a great fallback plan if we cannot agree. Most business owners know the value of their business best and an agreed-upon value works well. There are many things to consider in a buy/sell agreement, and we are going to go through the main areas that we talk about when we meet with business owners.

Death—Death is commonly looked at as the easiest way to solve because we can buy life insurance on my partners if they pass. However, we commonly see the titling of these policies to be incorrect, which can cause significant tax ramifications.

For example, in a partnership, if I pass away and $1 million goes to my company, the company then buys stock back from my wife. However, when my partner then goes to sell the business for $2 million, his basis may not have increased, resulting in taxation on the full $2 million of the business, assuming we had zero basis.

Vice versa, if it is a cross-purchase scenario where he gets the $1 million and then buys the stock from my wife, now it is as if he contributed $1 million to the company, and when he sells it for $2 million, he only pays taxes on the $1 million of additional growth, which saves my partner $150,000-$250,000 in taxes.

Having insurance is the easy scenario to buy the deceased partner out. But many times the term of the insurance has run out or one of the business owners is uninsurable. I gave the example of thirty days after a partner has passed away their spouse or beneficiaries need to be paid, which is very unrealistic and might be the detriment to the company. In some cases we would have to sell and liquidate, whether the remaining partners wanted to or not.

Having terms set up inside a buy/sell agreement upon passing to say we will pay you out over a certain time period with a certain interest is a much better fallback and protection for a company when properly structured insurance cannot be placed.

Disability—We all too often see disability listed in a document, and there is no real, good definition of disability. In some businesses a partner may do very little and are effectively an absentee owner. If that partner wants out and wants to liquidate and they claim disability, it can become very contentious. Maybe they should not have the ability to get out based on a generic definition of disability, because every company is different and the definition should correspond.

There is insurance to protect against the disability buyout; it can be very costly, but in some cases it is a very important piece to your business. But it is very important to have terms on how we buy out a disabled partner. For example, there is a 10 percent down payment and remainder over seven or ten years, depending on the cash flow of the company.

In one example, one business owner went out on disability overnight and their buy/sell agreement said upon death or disability they would be paid in full. It happened after their three best years, and they went to court. Because the signed agreement said if you are disabled you get to be bought out, the remaining partner then had to go out and borrow a significant sum of money at not-favorable interest rates to pay their partner off, and the partner was 50 percent of the revenue being produced.

Departure with and without Notice—Departure could be retirement, and how do I prepare for your buyout? How many hours or days do you have to work to remain my partner? If I am going to an island and I am just collecting a check, am I now considered retired? Is there a clause to force retirement? These questions state the importance of departure. There should also be an allotted time to give notice so I can prepare for the buyout.

Departure without notice is much more difficult for a business to handle. If I come in one day and say, "I am out of here; pay me." Commonly in documents we see that all the death, disability, retirement, or just leaving is treated the same way. Departure without notice is much more difficult for a business to handle. If I come in one day and say, "I am out of here; pay me now." This means you need to go borrow money immediately or use valuable cash on hand to buy me out. When we look at departure without notice, we typically want to disincentivize our partners from doing this. Therefore, we may suggest to discount your shares by 50 percent of the value and extend the payout to a ten-year term at the lowest applicable federal interest rates.

Transfer—Many Partners sign up to do business with the partner, not the spouse, ex-spouse, or children of their partners. Understanding how shares can transfer is important. You may want to allow shares to be transferred into a trust, as I mentioned earlier, by having a revocable trust or an irrevocable trust for estate tax planning. These trusts should have qualified Subchapter S trust provisions in case your business is an S Corporation. If not, the trust could have an adverse impact on the tax status for all the remaining partners.

Equalization—For example, a client passed away and was paid $6 million for the value of his business. The two partners agreed upon a value of $12 million. Six months after the passing, the remaining partner decided to sell. We ended up selling the business for $20 million, which, without equalization provisions, the partner of the family who passed would not have received an additional $4 million. Typically we will look at equalization over a twelve- or twenty-four-month period after a death, disability, and even retirement.

Force Out—How do you force out a partner? One should have the ability to force out an unproductive partner, and sometimes partners want to go in different directions. This also brings in the addition of a non-compete or non-solicitation agreement.

There is an upfront cost of having these documents and typically one of the reasons that business owners do not have them. Our recommendation is that while you are happy, healthy, and wealthy, invest in a good document as opposed to when something bad happens, when the business or the owners are under stress.

THE WRAP-UP

These scenarios that we spoke about in this chapter have been on a very high level analysis of considerations for a business owner. They also include numbers that will become irrelevant as tax laws change. As I said at the beginning, each one of these sections could have its own book. We were not able to touch on business succession and exit strategies, but for a free analysis and report of your business succession readiness, visit our website: www.academyfinancialinc.com and the link under Our Services, Business Owner Planning, BERI Survey.

This chapter is really the tip of the iceberg to hopefully drum up questions for the business owner to say, "Maybe this is something that I should be thinking about or doing."

Having an advisor that will look at your situation from a cross-disciplinary basis, not just from a personal or business perspective, but across the board, and having advisors that will bring creative design ideas and solutions to the table are very important to your financial success. Every successful business owner opens and welcomes creativity and unique designs, and those are the things that you should be getting from your current advisors or be seeking out to make sure you are optimizing what is most likely your greatest asset.

Professional Profile:

Michael McFeeley, CFP°, CRPC°, MSFS

Michael.McFeeley2@lfg.com | 410-339-6612 |

www.academyfinancialinc.com

A financial professional for nine years, Mike specializes in **Financial Planning for Successful Business Owners and their families**. Mike works on a cross-disciplinary basis to bring creative ideas to his clients in the form of business succession, estate, insurance, and financial independence planning.

Mike is a graduate of the United States Merchant Marine Academy, Kings Point, where he played football and baseball. After graduating, Mike served eight years in the Naval Reserve as a Lieutenant and worked as a Navigator on US Flag vessels for five years while obtaining his Master of Science degree in Financial Services from the American College.

Mike began at Academy Financial, Inc. in December of 2008 and became a Partner in 2011. Mike also became a member of The Resource Group in 2012. The Resource Group is comprised of the Top 200 planners in the country for Lincoln Financial Advisors. Mike is a member of Private Wealth Services and the Business Intelligent Institute, bringing business owners the advanced coordinated planning they need. Mike has also earned the CERTIFIED FINANCIAL PLANNER™ (CFP°) Practitioner certification, as well as the CRPC°, Certified Retirement Planning Counselor designation. Mike and Academy Financial have offices in Lutherville and Columbia, Maryland, as well as York, Pennsylvania, and Richmond and Vienna, Virginia.

Most Importantly, Mike lives in York, PA with his two children, Makayla and Michael, as well as his wonderful wife, Vanessa. Mike is an active member of Florida Citrus Sports and serves as a scout for the Citrus Bowl and is heavily involved in Orlando charities. Mike is also a member of the York Economic Alliance, helping grow York, PA business and community.

CHAPTER EIGHT

INVESTING DEMYSTIFIED

By Alex Harrison

INTRODUCTION

As an advisor for twenty years, I've run into many differing investment situations with many different clients. These scenarios run the gamut and include the retiree who almost has enough in personal assets to be "okay," the business owner who recently sold their business and needs to learn how to be an investor instead of a business owner, the executive that is accumulating for retirement, or the widow who has recently lost a loved one and is thrust into managing the family affairs. The personal circumstances vary, but investing is still very similar in each situation. Interestingly the goal is the same for most—financial security. In the pages that follow we will focus on what's important for most investors.

DEFINE INVESTING

If you spend a few minutes on Google, you can find multiple definitions for investing. Investopedia says that, "Investing is the act of committing money or capital to an endeavor (a business, project, real estate, etc.) with the expectation of obtaining an additional income or profit. Investing also can include the amount of time you put into the study of a prospective company or endeavor, especially since time is money." Merriam-Webster defines investing as, "the outlay of money usually for income or profit: capital outlay; *also*: the sum invested, or the property purchased." My definition of investing for this chapter— investing is managing personal capital to accomplish a purpose.

WHERE TO START

Many client situations we encounter are a mess when we are first introduced. They know this but don't know where to start. These scenarios can include many accounts across multiple investment firms, often with multiple investment advisors that have been opened at different times for different purposes. The first step can often be the hardest.

Take stock of your current financial situation; do an inventory of all the different bank accounts, 401(k)s, IRAs, investment accounts, UTMAs, etc. With this inventory you can begin comparing "what" you have with your goals. Don't be discouraged! This is just the starting line . . . You can get organized, and it won't be painful. Remember that going through this process is much easier than many of the other things you may dread (colonoscopy, root canal, etc.).

IDENTIFY YOUR GOALS

We all have the goal to be financially independent one day. This is the ability for a family to live off the earnings of their assets to support their financial needs and wants. Do you know how much it takes to "fund" your household for a month, or a quarter, or an entire year? Be specific and realistic; if your goal is to provide for your financial independence, then financial independence should be clearly defined.

What are the other reasons for investing? Goals-based planning is very popular and includes college funding, saving for a vacation home, providing an inheritance for your kids, and many others. Identifying your goals for investing will help you keep the main thing the main thing.

OUR PHILOSOPHY

We believe that wise investors have three things in common:

1. Prudent investors should be adequately compensated for the risks they assume.

2. Prudent investors should be positioned for a reasonable probability of success relative to their goals.

3. Prudent investors should not be exposed to potentially avoidable catastrophic risks.

We should break these down one by one. First, it is safe to say that an investor that is not willing to assume any risk is likely to achieve a low rate of return relative to inflation. In today's investment environment, money market returns are approximately 1-1.5 percent. Inflation is approximately 2 percent (core inflation), and as a result, an investor who positions their holdings all in cash or cash equivalents can expect to loss (purchasing power) 0.5-1 percent per year to inflation. This phenomenon is not new, as investors have historically underperformed inflation in cash, causing loss of purchasing power over time.

The "risk-free" rate of return is often measured as the ten-year treasury yield. Today that yield is 3 percent, which is historically low albeit not as low as we have become accustomed to in recent times. An investor who invests in treasury bonds at today's levels can expect to gain 1 percent above inflation. This assumes the investor holds the bond until maturity, pays no transaction or management fees, and isn't subject to income tax. Therefore, net of transaction fees, management expense, and taxes, most investors who own treasury bonds break even with inflation at best.

On the other side of the risk spectrum, an investor who invests solely in emerging markets or in a single stock is taking on an extreme amount of risk. Their expected return could be much higher than inflation over the long term, but in the short term they should buckle in for a wild ride. This high-risk approach is not recommended. Remember, investing 100 percent into any one position is probably a bad investment.

We measure if an investor is being compensated fairly for the risk they assume by the use of the efficient frontier. Efficient frontier is the rational way to diversify a portfolio to help you achieve the highest level of potential return for the risks you are willing to take. Significant differences exist in risk among investment asset classes. Risk is the variability of returns from an investment; the greater the variability, the greater the risk.

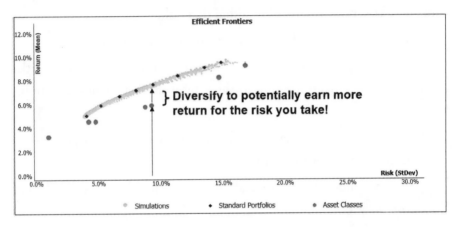

The blue diamonds represent efficiently diversified portfolios—the red dots are single asset classes. Notice that the blue diamonds have higher return than the red dots for given level of risk

ASSET ALLOCATION

Asset Allocation is the decision of how to invest a pool of resources among broad asset classes. The purpose of asset allocation is to help control risks by reducing the volatility (or degree of fluctuations) of your overall portfolio and help to optimize your total return (return on an investment that includes capital appreciation and interest or dividends).

An optimized portfolio seeks to maximize the potential portfolio return for a given level of risk. In other words, a principal goal is to deliver the maximum level of return per unit of risk through diversification into several asset classes.[1]

Why allocate assets? Asset allocation has been identified as the single most important element of investment success. According to a research, 90 percent or more of a portfolio's return and risk is driven by asset allocation. The remaining 10 percent comes from other sources such as security selection, active management, etc. Investors who do not properly diversify may take higher risks in their portfolio but may not earn higher returns to compensate them for taking that risk.[2]

Asset allocation provides three major benefits to an investor—

1. It provides a portfolio management discipline, which will help the investor to avoid reacting to short-term market swings, emotions, and fads.

2. It emphasizes the development of an asset allocation policy—an important factor for helping achieve investment returns.

3. When followed over several market cycles, it reduces risk and volatility.

Asset allocation is not a perfect solution—

• It cannot guarantee an investor will earn any given investment return.

• It is not as effective for short investment time horizons.

• It cannot eliminate all risks.

• It cannot guarantee a portfolio will never show a loss or have a losing year.

---

1 Source: Gary P. Brinson, L. Randolph Hood, and Gilbert T. Beebower. 1986. 'Determinants of Portfolio Performance.' Financial Analysts Journal, vol. 42. No. 4 (July/August 39-48).

2 Source: Roger G. Ibbotson and Paul D. Kaplan. 2000. 'Does Asset Allocation Explain 40, 90, or 100 Percent of Performance?' The Financial Analysts Journal

- It will not create a portfolio that will outperform a strong bull market

Making your portfolio efficient is only the first step. If you have the most efficient portfolio possible, with an 20 percent equity / 80 percent bond allocation, yet you need to achieve an 8 percent annualized rate of return to achieve your goal, the probability of accomplishing your goal is very low. In order to achieve your goal, your investment portfolio should be in line with the needed return to realize your goal. This is why investment planning should be part of your overall financial plan and not a stand-alone effort.

Avoiding potentially catastrophic risks seems easy, right? You'd be surprised. Many portfolios that we review are filled with potential risks that can be avoided. One of the most common is overexposure to one company stock. Most executives are paid in their employers' company stock. This perk is very helpful in the creation of wealth but requires prudence. Ask the employees of major banks about their company stock before and after 2008. Before 2008, I would hear comments like, "It's a bank; what could happen?" Post financial crisis, it was a completely different situation. Catastrophic risks can come in many forms; technology bubble, extreme valuations, and many others. I encourage you to work with your advisor to flush out any potential catastrophic risk exposures in your portfolio.

WHY ARE YOU INVESTING?

Financial independence is the ability to maintain your lifestyle on the earnings and withdrawal of the assets you own. This could be based on rental income, interest from bonds, dividends from stocks, or portfolio withdrawals that are sustainable. Investing to achieve financial independence can be very different from the process of maintaining financial independence. Once in retirement, cash flow is king!

Investing to provide an income in retirement can be challenging in today's low interest rate environment. The quagmire is rooted in the need for more income while not taking on too much risk. In order to achieve the higher income to support your retirement lifestyle, additional risk is necessary and can become a problem to an investor. Be careful not to take on too much risk while "chasing yield." Many high dividend/income stocks are trading at very high valuations today and don't come without risk. Remember, the old concept of risk vs. reward.

In order to achieve more return, more risk is required. One of my clients described the efficient frontier like the speedometer in an old GM car. If the "needle" is on the left we are sitting still, if the needle points all the way to the right we are speeding along the highway at eighty-five-plus miles per hour. Based on our experience, most investors are comfortable traveling at speeds between forty and seventy. The amount of risk you take will depend on the goal you are investing to accomplish and how much you worry about the ups and downs on the journey. Here are a several common goals-based investments for individual investors:

- Funding retirement
- Current income
- Education funding
- Dream home
- Family legacy

Let's dive into this in a little more detail with a couple of examples. If you are investing to fund educational goals for your child, his/her age is very important. While in elementary school, saving for college is over seven to twelve years away and is a long enough time period to take a long-term investment view. However, if your child is in eighth grade, the investments will need to be used in the next five to eight years. This will require a more conservative allocation because the time horizon is much shorter.

Matching the time horizon with the goal for your investments is essential for successful investing. A time horizon is the length of time over which an investment is made or held before it is liquidated. Time horizons can range from seconds, in the case of a day trader, to decades for a buy-and-hold investor or an individual who is investing in a retirement plan. Investment time horizons are determined by an investor's goals for the funds rather than the investment itself.

Another good example is retirement planning. While you are working and saving, at a young age retirement can seem like a lifetime away. At age thirty or thirty-five, an investor has a very long-term investment time horizon. One can expect not to utilize their retirement assets for at least twenty years and in most cases more than thirty years. A lot can change in thirty years. Thirty years ago, it was 1988 . . . Do you remember what you were doing in 1988? What were interest rates in 1988? How about stock market in 1987? The Dow Jones Industrial Average ended 1986 at 1895.95. Hindsight is twenty-twenty, and I'm sure many of us would like to go back and invest differently based on what we know now. If you are a long-term investor, remember that! Don't worry or fret about the short-term news of the day or current crisis. It's more important to stay invested than try to outsmart the markets in the short-term by trying to time when to get in and when to get out. Timing the markets doesn't work as an investment strategy.

As retirement approaches, it is important to begin to ready your retirement assets for this critical time. In the old days (when interest rates were near 5 percent for the ten-year treasury and life expectancy was shorter) this was a fairly easy task. Simply buy enough bonds to live on the 5 percent interest, and that was that. Fortunately, and unfortunately, these times have changed. Life expectancy has increased dramatically, and as demonstrated in this chart, at age sixty-five, retirees should expect to both live nearly twenty years in retirement with a high possibility of one living much longer.

Figure 1. Life expectancy at selected ages, by sex: United States, 2016 and 2017

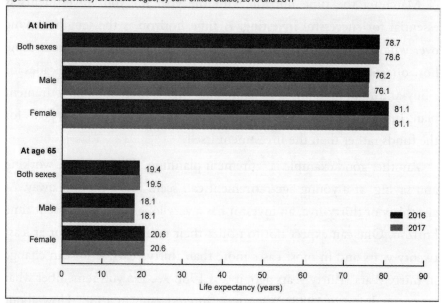

NOTES: Life expectancies for 2016 were revised using updated Medicare data; therefore, figures may differ from those previously published. Access data table for Figure 1 at: https://www.cdc.gov/nchs/data/databriefs/db328_tables-508.pdf#1.
SOURCE: NCHS, National Vital Statistics System, Mortality.

This means that part of the retirement assets must have a longer-term investment focus. In addition, with interest rates very low, it is increasingly more difficult to earn enough interest and/or dividends to simply live off the earnings of the portfolio. This creates a conundrum for investors and, in my opinion, warrants the use of an advisor to design the "right" answer for each investor. Every fact pattern I've encountered is different and results in fairly unique answers.

While the actual investment portfolios and holdings may be similar, the method of getting there can be extremely different. Let me use a quick medical analogy; as a cancer survivor, I can tell you that the chemotherapy and radiation treatment I have had was very standard. However, the fact pattern leading up to my treatment was very unique. Regardless of the standard treatment, I went to the experts at MD Anderson in Houston, Texas, to guide me through the process.

BEING REAL ABOUT RISK

Risk is defined as the chance an investment's actual return will differ from the expected return. Risk includes the possibility of losing some or all of the original investment. Different versions of risk are usually measured by calculating the standard deviation of the historical returns or average returns of a specific investment. This can be measured in many ways. For me, risk is best described when the value of a portfolio goes down. I know that I had X in my account, and now I have less than X.

It doesn't feel good or make us happy to see our account values lower at any point in time. In the perfect world, an investment account would go up every year by some amount that is fair and never go down until I need to start withdrawing from the account.

I don't know many people who have figured out how to live life without risk. As I write this, I'm on a plane heading home from Houston. We drove a car to the airport in order to board the plane and ate lunch at the airport before boarding our flight. All of these items come with risk: plane crash, car crash, and food poisoning, to mention a few. But we are familiar with accepting the risks that come from our daily life. For some reason, our risk attitude changes when it comes to our investments.

I have met some who don't even look at their statements and are comfortable taking on investment risk. Then I've met others that are so risk averse they will only invest in "guaranteed" types of investments. Many think that investing in US treasury bonds is guaranteed. While very secure, I could make the argument that there is still risk in the actual risk-free investment.

Behavioral finance is a subject that has many experts. I am not one of those experts with a PhD in economics, but I can share with you a couple things I have learned. We all have a tendency to believe that the investment markets will continue in the direction they are now heading, indefinitely. When that direction is down, no one wants to invest, and everyone that's in gold or cash is an "expert."

When that direction is up, we have an insatiable appetite for risk. We can't invest enough. I like to use Warren Buffet's saying: "When everyone is fearful, I will be greedy, but when everyone is greedy, I become fearful."

The best way I have found to manage risk is to remember why you're investing. If you keep your goal in mind, it makes the journey worth the effort and will likely prevent you from making bad decisions. Over the long term, the goal is to make more good decisions than bad decisions.

Time is your friend when investing. John Bogle says, "Time is your friend. Start early, stick to a plan, and ignore the chatter of the day. Let the miracle of compound interest work for you" (John Bogle's 10 Key Rules of Investing, 2014). If things don't go well in the beginning, don't panic. Stick with the plan.

Along the way it is important to measure your success. Are you still on track to accomplish your goal? Reviewing your progress and making sure that you still have a reasonable probability of reaching your destination is the most important yard stick to compare against. Some folks believe that comparing a portfolio to a benchmark like the S&P 500 or Dow Jones Industrial Average is the only way to measure success.

I submit that achieving your goal is more important than outperforming an arbitrary benchmark. And please note that those benchmarks make no mention of the key element I mentioned earlier: risk.

Comparing your investment holdings to an appropriate benchmark is human and done daily by many, but remember there are multiple factors to consider to understand the full picture. Risk, costs, manager tenure, and others are very important. In some cases, active management does outperform passive (or index) investing. One good example of this outperformance can be seen in emerging market funds.

Many of the mutual funds in that category have significantly outperformed the standard emerging market index. There are plenty of good resources available (such as Morningstar) to help evaluate the performance of funds. Personally, I compare my investment results to my goal and appropriate blended benchmarks annually. I have found that increasing the frequency that I review my accounts doesn't necessarily impact the outcome; it just increases the stress level. Warren Buffet says it best, "Successful investing takes time, discipline, and patience. No matter how great the talent or effort, some things just take time; you can't produce a baby in one month by getting nine women pregnant."

DOING IT ALONE

Investment management can be accomplished in different ways: with an advisor alongside to help, with a computer alongside to help, or on your own. Any of these solutions will work, but for the best outcome I suggest you consider a few things. First, are you coachable? Are you the type of person that likes to get advice from your accountant before the end of the year about your income tax planning?

We have found that people who are coachable and like to get advice before making major decisions fair best when having an advisor provide guidance for the best options in investment management. Conversely, if you are the type person to read a book and implement your interpretation of the book without discussing it with others, you are more likely to feel better investing on your own. There is no right or wrong answer here . . . It's all about how comfortable you are in the process and keeping your eye on the goal.

SUMMARY

Investing is simple but not easy. The basics include taking stock of the resources, identifying the goal, measuring the time available to accomplish the goal, and determining how bumpy of a ride you can tolerate. One of the most important tools that all good investors possess is a detachment of emotion from their investments. Like many aspects of our lives, emotions can cloud our judgement and lead to poor decision making.

One advantage I have as an advisor to successful families is the luxury of bringing a pragmatic, unemotional approach to the management of our clients' wealth. This allows me to ask the hard questions and, in some cases, come up with more practical answers to emotionally driven concerns.

Recently a client was in my office discussing a real concern about beginning her withdrawals from retirement accounts. We had planned for this day for nearly a dozen years, and I thought that she would be excited to hear that her investments would easily support her desired standard of living. Our brilliant planning and mathematically based stewardship had led to prudent decisions through the financial crisis and to this very day. What was I missing? To my surprise, she mentioned a real desire to provide a sizable inheritance to her daughter. This goal was preventing her from feeling good about enjoying her wealth. Wow! I had completely missed that goal, and her emotional connection to the inheritance was impacting her ability to make a good decision. Through a meaningful conversation, we were able to come up with a solution that would provide for her daughter and allowed her to begin receiving the retirement income she had worked so hard to accumulate.

Investing allows us the opportunity to live our lifestyles, educate our children, take care of our parents, leave a legacy for our children, and give back to our communities. Most of the time, investing is simply a means to an end. It's a discipline that requires wisdom, prudence, and patience.

Professional Profile:

Alexander P. Harrison

Alex.Harrison@LFG.com | 904-380-4015 |

www.AlexHarrison.com

Alexander P. Harrison has more than twenty years of experience working exclusively with executives, professionals, and business owners. The Florida native specializes in estate and gift planning, financial independence, investment planning, employee stock option analysis, wealth accumulation, insurance analysis, and business succession planning.

Alex is a graduate of the Coggin College of Business at the University of North Florida, with a Bachelor of Business Administration degree, majoring in Financial Services. He is also a Registered Financial Consultant (RFC) with Lincoln Financial Advisors Corp. and an avid student of the business.

Additionally, Alex is a "Prestige Member" of Sagemark Consulting Private Wealth Services (SPWS), a preeminent group of financial planners within Lincoln Financial Advisors Corp. who possess exceptional experience. The "Serve First" philosophy is evident within this group of practitioners. With extensive experience working with large corporations and their executives, Alex's unique expertise allows him to work closely with advisors and clients around the country.

As a survivor of oral cancer, Alex knows what's really important: faith, family, friends. Empathy, wisdom, and situational awareness are critical characteristics that Alex possesses and leads for his team. The Jacksonville, Florida, resident is married to Kami, and they have two children, Kinley and Maguire.

CHAPTER NINE

CORPORATE RETIREMENT PLANS—MAKE SURE IT'S A GOOD FIT

By J. Louis McCraw & Tyler R. McCraw

TO IMPLEMENT OR NOT TO IMPLEMENT

Regardless of how much money we make or how much we love our work, at some point we all look forward to retirement. Yes, it may be with some degree of trepidation, and the vision of retirement may differ for each of us. But let's face it, time and tide wait for no man. Age catches up with us all; yes—even you!

As a business owner or key person in a company, the business is part of your makeup. You live and breathe it each day; that is all good. I get it.

Odds are, no matter how loyal and true your employees may be, they and their families value their ability to retire. Therefore, if you wish to attract and retain employees, a qualified retirement plan is an essential element in the success of your company. An employee that feels financially secure is more productive and will remain a long-term employee.

In this chapter we will discuss how to design a plan to fit with your objectives and budget. We will identify methods by which the IRS allows you to provide attractive benefits for you and your key employees on a tax-favorable basis.

Before we go forward, I want you to identify the objectives you wish to achieve. Our clients have utilized retirement plans to accomplish one or more of the following objectives:

- To attract and retain employees
- To reward owners
- To reward key employees
- To reduce taxes
- To pre-fund the buyout of the owner

DESIGN

As with any other business project you undertake, you need to identify the purpose or objective you wish to accomplish by implementing a retirement plan for your organization. Your advisor, along with your Third Party Administrator (TPA), should be able to assist you in formulating your ideas.

With any business project, it is always about the money, or at least, the trade-offs. All decisions eventually affect the bottom line. Before you make an outlay of corporate dollars to fund a retirement plan, you need to consider:

- Cash Flow—Can we commit to an outlay each year, or is there too much ebb and flow in our revenue?

- Source—Depending upon the plan type, the primary source for funding may be the employer, the employee, or a combination of both.

- Crawl First / Walk Later—If you are a new company or adopting a plan for the first time, you may want to avoid a financial commitment and retain as much flexibility in the funding as possible. It is always easier to enhance plan benefits later than to overreach and be forced to reduce employees' benefits.

- Demographics—What is the age of your employees and how does this relate to the age of the owners? If the owner is fifty plus years of age, and the employees are primarily in their forties or younger, you may be able to heavily favor the owners or key employees. The size of your employee group may impact your decision. A plan design that fits an employer with fifty employees may be cost prohibitive for an employer with 500 employees.

PLAN TYPES

Before you consider adopting or modifying your current plan, it is essential that you have a general working knowledge of the various plan types available to you.

A good advisor with in-depth knowledge of retirement plans or a third-party administrator (TPA) is your best source for information and guidance.

Yes, basic plan design is "off the rack." Be sure the plan you implement fits your objectives, cash flow, and the culture of your organization. There are numerous tweaks and steps that can be taken to "tailor fit" your plan. Let's start with the basics in helping you to understand plan design.

The two major families of plans are *Defined Contribution* and *Defined Benefit*.

DEFINED CONTRIBUTION PLANS—

This is by far the most widely used family of plans. All profit-sharing and 401(k) plans fit into this category. There are several other types but they go beyond the scope of our discussion. In defined contribution (DC) plans, the employees' benefit is their ending account balance, and the employees assume the risk of return.

Unlike pension plans, profit-sharing plans provide employers with flexibility. Under a profit-sharing plan, the employer may or may not make a contribution at their

discretion. A profit-sharing plan document must define the allocation formula or how contributions to employee accounts will be determined.

Also, it is important to note that the name "profit sharing" is misleading. The employer's contribution is not linked to the profits and may vary year to year at the employer's discretion, even zero in a windfall year.

The Internal Revenue Code (IRC) Section 401(k) defines the rules for salaried deferral plans. For some reason the paragraph section became the name we all know for the most often-utilized plan.

Think of 401(k) plans as an overlay on a profit-sharing plan that permits employees to make salaried deferrals. Good plan design dictates that the plan document include profit-sharing language whenever adopting a 401(k) plan, even if the employer never intends to make any employer contributions. The profit-sharing portion can remain dormant until needed.

A 401(k) plan is usually the least expensive plan for the employer. The plan may be employee funded only, or the employer may elect to make matching as well as profit-sharing contributions. We will discuss these options under the Plan Evolution section.

DEFINED BENEFIT PLANS—

The defined benefit (DB) plan is a type of pension plan and favors older employees. Unlike profit-sharing plans, in which the employer has the flexibility to make or not make contributions in a plan year, the pension plan is a fixed obligation. This requires that the employer have a predictable cash flow.

The employee retirement benefit is determined by a formula typically based upon compensation and the number of years employed. For example, 2 percent of the highest five years of compensation, multiplied by years of services. Or it may be a more basic formula: 50 percent of the average of the three highest years of compensation. The formula can take on many different looks. Typically, your actuary will back into the benefit formula based on your budget and employee demographics.

In a DB Plan, the employer has made a promise to the employee to provide an income at retirement of a specified dollar amount or a lump sum equal to the present value of the stream of income payments. Therefore the return of risk is assumed by the employer, not the employee as in the DC plans.

If the rate of return on the assets is greater than the projected rate, for example 6 percent, the employer funding requirement is reduced. However if the rate of return is lower, contribution requirements will be greater in order to fund the promised benefit.

For many years, employees of Fortune 500 companies enjoyed the assurance of the guaranteed retirement income offered by defined benefit plans. With the downturn in the economy and the stock market slide earlier this decade, many of the large corporations, especially in the automobile industry, could no longer afford to provide such a strong retirement benefit.

In recent years we have seen the defined benefit plan reemerge in popularity among privately held companies. Defined benefit plans are an excellent method for a smaller employer to shelter tax dollars for the owner or key employees.

CASH BALANCE PLANS—

A cash balance (CB) plan is a type of defined benefit plan with a defined contribution flavor. A CB plan maintains a hypothetical individual employee account similar to a defined contribution plan. Under the plan, the employer contributes a percentage of the employee's compensation plus a set interest rate of 5 or 6 percent is credited to the account annually. Financial risk and investment risk are assumed by the employer as in any defined benefit plan.

After reaching a decision on the most suitable plan design for you and your company, your TPA will prepare a plan document for your plan. A plan document is required by the IRS for all qualified plans in order to receive a deduction. This document will outline all the plan rules, ranging from eligibility, to vesting, to the allocation formula, and will dictate the specific operations of your plan.

PLAN EVOLUTION

The earlier paragraphs have provided you with an insight to the various types of plans. Now I want you to determine where you and your organization are along the evolution timeline. Again, the key factors are:

- Budget
- Cash flow
- Objectives

401(k) No Match: This is the basic no-frills approach. If you are a start-up or adopting a plan for the first time, this may be suitable for you. It is 100 percent employee funded. The employer may elect to pay the administration fees or have the fees deducted from the plan assets.

401(k) with Employer Match: Step one in the evolutionary process involves making an employer match as an incentive for employees to defer.

This may be achieved with a minimum additional cost. For example, a twenty-five cents per dollar match on the first 4 percent deferred is equivalent to 1 percent of payroll. Therefore, you know your maximum exposure if all employees contribute at the 4 percent rate or greater. The matching formula should be discretionary with the ability to be changed with advance notice to the employees.

401(k) Testing: Let's take a step back and discuss two compliance tests that may impact your 401(k):

1. Average Deferral Percentage Test and

2. Top Heavy

For testing purposes, employees are divided into Highly Compensated Employees (HCE) and Non-Highly Compensated Employees (NHCE).

A HIGHLY COMPENSATED EMPLOYEE (HCE) IS DEFINED AS:

- Owner of more than 5 percent, including attribution rules to include spouse, children, grandchildren, and parents, or

- An employee with compensation in excess of a specified limit ($125,000 for 2019), or if favorable for testing, the employer may define HCEs as the top 20 percent of employees based on compensation

Average Deferral Percentage (ADP) Test: The IRS wants to assure that not just the top employees are benefiting from a 401(k) plan. The ADP test compares the deferrals made by the HCE to deferrals of NHCE. HCE deferrals must fit into the following ranges:

NHCE Deferral Avg.	HCE Avg. Deferral Limit
2% or less	NHCE % x 2
2% to 8%	NHCE % + 2
> 8%	NHCE x 1.25%

TOP HEAVY RULES: (WWW.IRS.GOV/RETIREMENT-PLANS)

A plan is considered Top Heavy when the total of the key employee accounts exceeds 60 percent of the total plan assets. A "key" employee is defined as anyone who:

A) Has more than 5 percent ownership in the company.

B) Owns more than 1 percent of the company and receives compensation of more than $150,000/year (2019 limit).

C) Is an officer of the company and receives compensation greater than $180,000 (2019 limit).

If a plan is Top Heavy, the employer generally must make up to a 3 percent of compensation contribution for each eligible non-key employee. Also a minimum vesting schedule is required.

A number of years ago, the IRS realized that regardless of how much they may try, privately held business owners could not always persuade their employees to contribute to their 401(k) plan. This restricted the owners and highly compensated employees in the amount they could defer. In many instances the owner decided to not have a plan at all, which hurt everyone. As a safe measure against this action, the IRS implemented a revision known as safe harbor.

Safe Harbor Plans – A safe harbor 401(k) plan is our most popular plan design.

By making a minimal contribution to all employees, a plan is considered a safe harbor plan and may avoid the Average Deferral Percentage (ADP) and Top Heavy tests. Many employers opt to implement a safe harbor plan to be exempt from the above tests, assuring the highly compensated employees will be able to maximize their salary deferrals. A plan is considered a safe harbor plan if it adopts one of the following:

A—Safe Harbor Match: The basic safe harbor match is $1.00 per dollar on the first 3 percent deferred, plus $.50 on the next 2 percent deferred by the employee. The employee receives a 4 percent match if they defer 5 percent or more. An **enhanced** safe harbor match is dollar for dollar on the first 4 percent of deferral.

B—Three Percent Non-Elective Safe Harbor: All eligible employees receive a 3 percent employer contribution regardless if they make a deferral to the plan. Note that all safe harbor contributions must be 100 percent vested immediately.

Profit Sharing: To enhance the employee's benefit and/or to reduce taxes, an employer may wish to make an additional employer contribution known as a profit-sharing allocation. Again, a profit-sharing contribution is discretionary and may range from zero to 25 percent of the eligible employees' payroll. The 25 percent limit does not include 401(k) deferrals made by the employees.

Allocation Formula: As mentioned earlier, a profit-sharing plan does not require a contribution. However, the plan document must contain an allocation formula outlining how employer contributions will be allocated to the employees.

The most popular are:

- **Pro Rata**—The contribution equals the same percentage of compensation for all employees.

- **Integrated**—All employees receive a contribution equal to the same percentage of compensation, plus employees earning higher than the Social Security taxable wage base of $132,900 (2019 limit) may receive an additional contribution of up to 5.7 percent of their compensation in excess of the Social Security taxable wage base.

- **New Comparability** or **Cross-Tested** formulas permit all employees to be placed in separate job classifications for the purpose of allocating contributions. This can be especially advantageous for companies with older key employees or companies with many partners, such as a law firm or a medical practice.

DESIGN—OPTIMUM UTILIZATION

Over the years, we have had the opportunity to work with many different organizations and privately owned companies. Structuring the proper plan design has made a significant difference in satisfying their objectives and enabling them to provide retirement benefits on a tax-deductible basis to all employees and especially the key employees.

REAL-LIFE EXAMPLES:

EXAMPLE 1—NEW COMPARABILITY PROFIT-SHARING ALLOCATION

We were introduced to a law firm with fifty-six Partners and nearly as many staff employees. Each of the Partners ranged in ages from just out of law school to early seventies. The Firm had in place a 401(k) profit sharing with an integrated allocation formula.

Each of the Partners were in a different financial stage of life with different financial objectives. The younger Partners were still paying school loans, the middle-aged Partners had children attending college with high tuition bills, and the senior Partners were trying to maximize their tax deduction or perhaps catch up on the funding of their retirement benefits. Their current plan required each participant to receive basically the same percentage of compensation as a PS allocation.

Each year would lead to heated arguments over the amount to be contributed to the profit-sharing plan versus paid out in annual bonuses. We met with their board and introduced to them the new comparability profit-sharing allocation formula.

Utilizing the new comparability formula, we were able to place each of the Partners as well as each of the staff/employees in separate job classifications. This permitted each Partner to elect the amount they would receive in profit sharing each year compared to their bonus.

For example, if the bonus amount was to be $30,000, the Partner could elect to have all $30,000 allocated to their profit-sharing account or have a portion allocated to the profit sharing and receive the remainder in a cash bonus. This enabled the Senior Partners to maximize their retirement funding at $56,000 (2019 limit) or $62,000 if age fifty plus.

The $56,000 and $62,000 limits consist of a maximum employee 401(k) deferral of $19,000 (2019 limit) for employees under fifty, or $25,000 for employees fifty plus, plus any employer contributions.

The new comparability allocation formula enabled each Partner to satisfy their own funding objective through their 401(k) deferral and PS allocation without impacting the other Partners.

In addition, the Practice could elect to reward top-performing employees with a PS amount different from the other employees. All employees received a minimum profit-sharing contribution of 5 percent of compensation to satisfy compliance testing, including a 3 percent non-elected safe harbor contribution, which provided the Partners the flexibility to maximize their 401(k) deferral.

EXAMPLE 2—BUSINESS TRANSITION

I asked one of our business-owner clients about his plans for retirement. He was age sixty-four and planned on working until age seventy. Although age seventy still seemed like a distant date for him, it was essential we begin his transition into retirement almost immediately. Ideally, a business owner should begin transitioning into retirement at least over a five-year period, if possible, to obtain the best value and to transition the business smoothly. This would provide a suitable period for the younger, key employees he had identified as buyers to benefit from his guidance in assuming the reins of the company.

Upon further discussion, the owner shared with me that the business had accumulated cash in their corporate account and anticipated good cash flow for the foreseeable future. I suggested that we implement a cash balance plan that would enable him to pull money out of the corporation for his benefit without triggering a taxable event.

By combining a cash balance plan with their existing 401(k) new comparability profit-sharing plan, the corporation was able to make an additional contribution each year of $250,000 of which approximately $225,000 was allocated to the owner. Over a four-year period we were able to channel just over 1 million dollars into the owner's retirement account through the cash balance plan.

Now he is sixty-eight, the transition plan is operating smoothly, and he has been able to reduce the value of the company a million dollars, making it easier for the younger, key employees to purchase the company. Meanwhile he has been able to shelter a million dollars into his own retirement plan as a safety net in the event that the new owners are not able to fulfill their commitments.

EXAMPLE 3—REWARDING EMPLOYEES FOR EXCEPTIONAL PERFORMANCE

By establishing separate job classifications for all employees, a new comparability plan may enable you to reward your employees with profit-sharing contributions differing in percentages (again, this will be subject to testing). If all employees receive a 3 percent safe harbor (non-elective) contribution, you may be able to reward all the key employees with up to an additional 6 percent of compensation contribution. You may also elect to reward selected non-key employees even more.

A number of our clients have found this as an attractive method to reward employees for outstanding performance. Supervisors are often rewarded for exceeding production levels, or Project Managers, for completing a project before a deadline or under budget.

EXAMPLE 4—AVOIDING HIGHLY COMPENSATED LIMITATIONS

Due to testing limitations, you may not be able to reward HCEs beyond the 3 percent or 5 percent contribution you are contributing for all employees. This was the situation one of our business owners faced. The owner and I met with the two managers that were on target to earn $125,500 and $126,500.

We asked if they would be willing to cap their salary and bonus to $124,000. Of course at first they were not too excited about the idea until we explained that the owner would make a contribution of $7,000 for each of them under the profit-sharing plan.

By capping their compensation at $124,000 they were able to receive a greater total compensation package than they would have as highly compensated employees.

ADVISOR

As a business owner you wear many hats. Your day is full with the responsibility of the overall operation of your company. As important as a 401(k) or qualified plan is to your employees, it is not your primary focus. You should have an advisor to keep you apprised of all aspects of the plan. The advisor is your "quarterback" who will coordinate all activities and interact with your TPA to assure your plan is properly designed.

An experienced advisor is essential. There is just too much information and constantly changing compliance issues for you to risk trying to do this on your own. It will be difficult for you to keep abreast of industry trends. Your advisor should be keeping you abreast of best practices such as auto-enrollment, auto-increases, or plan designs that may be more in keeping with your objectives.

Be careful of what we refer to as the *Two-Plan Dan*. Two-Plan Dans are financial advisors or brokers that will seek out a 401(k) or retirement plan just for the assets only. They do not understand plan design and compliance issues. All too often, Two-Plan Dans are selected because of a personal relationship they may have with you or someone else in your firm.

They could be a golf buddy, a relative, or a good friend. Do you really want to trust your employees' retirement future to a person who has little or no experience in the overall complexities of qualified plans?

EDUCATIONAL MEETINGS—

Your advisor should be readily available to you and your employees. You should expect the advisor to provide educational meetings on a quarterly, semi-annual, or annual basis. The frequency will depend upon the needs of your employees and how often you are willing to remove your employees from the job site in order to have a forty-five-minute to one-hour meeting.

The advisor should be able to assist your employees in understanding portfolio structure and designing a portfolio suitable to their risk and objectives. Consider offering both group sessions as well as one-on-one meetings for the best results.

The primary focus of the educational meetings should be to assist the employees in understanding the amount of money they will need to retire, establishing objectives, and creating action steps to obtain their goals.

Most employees underestimate the amount of money they will need for retirement. They do not understand inflation and how inflation will erode their purchasing power. It is critical that they do not procrastinate, but get started TODAY!

The average salary deferral by an employee ranges from 5 percent to 7 percent of compensation. This is not nearly enough to be able to maintain their standard of living during retirement. The amount of savings each person will need to save in order to reach their retirement goals is different. Many factors will come into play. A good goal is to strive to invest 12 percent to 14 percent of compensation, including employer contributions, beginning at age thirty to maintain their standard of living during retirement.

CREDENTIALS

Though credentials do not assure competency, we suggest you see advisors who hold industry designations, such as the CERTIFIED FINANCIAL PLANNER™ (CFP®) designation or Chartered Financial Consultant (ChFC) or Chartered Retirement Planning Consultant (CRPC).

The advisor should be able to relate to your employees and assist them in simplifying the planning process. Most employees do not understand beta and downside capture. However, the right advisor can assist the employee in structuring a program in which they are comfortable and will help them to reach their goals.

If possible, select an advisory team to work with you and your employees. It is difficult for one person to be able to do all things and relate to all employees. With an advisory team, you will have two to four people who can work with your employees to provide more extensive services.

A good advisor should also understand beneficiary issues. The most common errors committed by employees are:

- Failure to complete a beneficiary form.
- Leaving money outright to children under the age of eighteen, or
- Failing to properly identify stepchildren and therefore accidently disinheriting a child they had intended to provide benefits.

Summary

Qualified retirement plans due to the IRS regulations and compliance testing have many complexities. Do not let the complexities prevent you from utilizing a plan to benefit you and your employees. An experienced advisor and TPA can assist you in navigating through the hurdles you face in obtaining your objectives.

Hopefully, in this brief chapter we have provided you with insight into how retirement plans may assist you to:

- Attract and retain employees
- Reward key employees in your organization
- Enhance the retirement experience for you and your employees
- Ease the transition of ownership of the company

Professional Profile:

J. Louis McCraw, MBA, CFP®, ChFC, CRPC®

LMcCraw@PFGAdvisors.net | 610-727-4949 |

www.PFGAdvisors.net

Lou is the founding partner of PFG Advisors, which formed in 2005. He has serviced clients in all aspects of financial planning since 1984. As a true specialist in the qualified plan market, he currently advises on over one hundred company-sponsored retirement plans, providing invaluable advice to both business owners and their employees.

In 1984, Lou founded Pension & Financial Services, Inc., a third-party administration firm. Lou served as the CEO of PFS until 2012 when he sold the firm. The twenty-eight years at the helm of a TPA provided him with the experience and insight into the plan design issues and complexities involved in the operations of qualified retirement plans.

Lou has earned industry certifications and designations of: CERTIFIED FINANCIAL PLANNER™ (CFP® certification), Chartered Financial Consultant (ChFC®), Chartered Life Underwriter (CLU®), and Chartered Retirement Planning Consultant (CRPC®).

Since 1992, Lou has continuously achieved the top honor of Chairman's Council within the Lincoln Financial Advisors network for his financial services within the community. In 2008 he received the Legacy Award from Lincoln Financial Advisors in recognition of his leadership and dedication to the industry.

Outside of work, Lou enjoys playing golf, exercising, and traveling. He and his wife, Linda, live in Malvern, Pennsylvania, and have three children, Shannon, Tyler and Logan.

Professional Profile:
Tyler R. McCraw, CFP°

Tyler.McCraw@LFG.com | 610-727-4904 |
www.PFGAdvisors.net

Tyler McCraw is a financial planner with PFG Advisors, serving personal wealth management clients and privately owned businesses throughout the Philadelphia area. Tyler firmly believes in the view of comprehensive planning first working with individual clients.

When working with privately owned businesses, Tyler focuses on qualified retirement plans. He has been associated with Lincoln Financial Advisors since the summer of 2012. With over ten years in the financial industry, Tyler previously worked in sales for two years with BlackRock and over four years with Lincoln Financial Distributors.

Tyler received his bachelor's degree from The College of William & Mary in 2006 and holds his Series, 7, 63, and 66 FINRA Registrations. He also holds a CERTIFIED FINANCIAL PLANNER™ certification (CFP° certification).

After playing four years of collegiate baseball at William & Mary, Tyler has remained active in the sports world and now resides in Berwyn, PA, with his wife, Lindsay, and two children.

CHAPTER TEN

USING LIFE INSURANCE IN FINANCIAL PLANS

By Derek B. Ferriera

Over the years I have been in the business, I have had the opportunity to experience the power of life insurance in a number of different ways. In some of these situations, the absence of life insurance was starkly evident in terms of what it would have done to change the outcome of the family for many generations after if it had been in existence.

One of the stories that comes to mind which comes up frequently over the years is from when I first entered the profession in the mid-eighties. One of the first clients I met, in fact, in the first week in business, had a small life insurance policy and wanted a review. After a few minutes of discussion, we realized that George was underinsured for family income loss. In other words, George, in this case, was the main bread earner, Janet was a stay-at-home mom, they had two children, and George was a hard-working man with a blue-collar job in California.

We underwrote an application, and in those days, we did what we called a binder, which means they put a good faith deposit down on the policy until it was completely underwritten for health, at which time it would go into force. The binder is a good faith deposit that insures the client temporarily by the insurance company while they are going through the underwriting process.

I collected one-month deposit on the insurance, and I tossed it in my briefcase and went to my office. A couple of hours later I had a message on my machine from Janet, who said that George had had a heart attack that night and was in the hospital not doing well. I gave her my best wishes and told her to keep me posted.

I got another call the next day saying that George had died the night before. I had not even finished formally filling out the application and had not submitted it or the check. Being new to the business, I went to my manager and asked what I should do. He said the binder was collected properly and I was to complete the application and submit it and then immediately explain what happened to the insurance company.

Long story short, after about a month of the insurance company doing their normal due diligence, they paid a claim of $500,000 in life insurance. I delivered that check to Janet for one-half-million dollars. The short story there is that Janet, with that money being invested and properly managed, was provided enough income that she did not have to go back to work and was able to continue to put her children through trade school, and they were able to remain in their house and not upheave their lifestyle or force their children to move away from their friends.

That was an amazing and stark introduction into my profession, given I had just started the business and was totally green behind the ears. I had just experienced the stark power and beauty of life insurance and what it can mean to a family (unfortunately in a very emotional way). This immediately gave me conviction for the rest of my career as to why life insurance should at least be discussed in every financial plan.

With the Computer Age we live in today, I believe very few people understand the different chassis of life insurance that exist or how and where they best fit into a financial plan, which I will discuss in more detail later.

Decades ago, life insurance used to be quoted and sold with using a book. Insurance companies would issue a rate book to its agents, and rates were based on a person's age and sex. This was known as whole life insurance, and somebody would calculate with a calculator a dollar rate per thousands of life insurance coverage, and an insured would pay that rate for life.

A portion of the premium would be allocated to a guaranteed death benefit and secondly as equity in the form of cash value. This equity could be accessed in an emergency or commonly used as a retirement supplement for a client should they need it.

It was very simplistic; it credited a low but guaranteed interest rate, usually 1 to 4 percent, perhaps, that could also be enhanced through the insurance company crediting additional dividends to the policy. It was a dual savings and protection vehicle for a family. As the Computer Age came about in the eighties, companies began to create more complex products with added flexibility and more transparency to meet consumer demands.

That has ultimately led to where we are today, where there are many different types of hybrid chassis available to fit many different circumstances for both family and business needs. Because of that, it is a much more complex world to shop for insurance and for an advisor to match the best design and chassis to a particular client's needs.

One of the things we hope to do in this chapter is to peel the lid off the black box of insurance and try to provide general parameters to allow you to break out the right type for the right situation and make it easier for you to match up the best product for the need and combination of facts put forth.

With better technology and better medical care, the mortality tables have been adjusted as people are living longer and the cost of insurance has actually decreased.

The insurance company uses mortality tables, which publish longevity rates for people in the US as a foundation for calculating odds and timing of the average death for a particular age, sex, and smoking or non-smoking combination. Premiums are designed to make enough profit to satisfy their shareholders and, while providing this created funding need to the consumers, still be competitive enough in the pricing environment to sell enough policies to the consumers that buy them.

When I first started in the business, insurance companies were pricing policies based on the 1958 mortality tables. In those days, the average male might be living to age seventy, and if you were a smoker you lived on average perhaps three to four less years than that. Females would live three or four years longer than males, and being a smoker resulted in similar reduction in average life as males.

Today we are dealing with a mortality table from 2010, with many companies poised to switch to the 2017 as their new products are released. People are living much longer, and this has made current insurance pricing lower. If you are going to live ten or fifteen years longer on average today than somebody at the same age back in the eighties, then the pricing can be less even though you are older, because the insurance company does not need to pay that claim on odds for many more years and prices accordingly. Increased transparency of fees and expense has also had a downward effect on pricing.

This phenomenon in today's marketplace is one that a lot of people are not aware of. To use the analogy that is easy to understand, about half the consumers today can replace their existing life insurance policy of years ago and decrease their premiums!

In essence, they can refinance their insurance by basically going through another physical and getting a policy with a better mortality table and more efficient underlying expense factors than when they bought their original insurance.

What every consumer should be doing is dusting off their policies and having a very thorough review to see if the newer mortality tables might be to their benefit. Many times they can obtain a new policy with more transparency, flexibility, and lower fee structures than their old policies had. When reviewing options, it's important to consider any fees that might be associated with the replacement of an older policy (i.e., surrender charges).

HOW TO IDENTIFY AND SELECT THE CORRECT CHASSIS

Thanks to the power of computers, the industry has gradually built more and more products that emphasize transparency and flexibility. But at its most fundamental, insurance runs the continuum nowadays from things that play with the variability and the risk of three components.

Those three components are premium, death benefit, and cash value equity, as well as who takes the risk on each of those three components.

Premium is the dollars paid to the insurance company for the policy.

Death benefit is the amount of monies paid by the insurance company to the beneficiary upon the death of the insured.

The cash value is the equity that builds up in the policy that is available to withdraw, loan, or surrender for cash during the lifetime of the insured and is accessible pre-death. The risk is either going to be at the insurance companies' level or the policyholder's level. Depending on who is taking that risk, how much, and how those three components are treated dictates the types of chassis that exist.

On one extreme you have term insurance, which is perhaps the easiest type to understand; it is very similar to homeowner's or auto insurance in the sense that a policyholder pays a premium and it is adjusted on a year-to-year basis, although many of them have hybrid guarantee periods for ten, fifteen, or twenty years to make it easier for shopping comparison and cash flow planning. If you die, it pays the death benefit income tax free. If you do not die, the policy expires and it goes away in the first year premiums are not paid.

Nobody returns any money to the policy holder and no money is due to the insurance company. It is essentially year-by-year coverage. This is frequently and most commonly used for people who have tight cash flow and a very short-term need for the insurance. On the other extreme, you have something called traditional or interest-sensitive whole life, which is the closest chassis available to policies when insurance began.

Every variable, the premium, the death benefit, and the cash value are all guaranteed to the insured. The interest rate credited to the cash value has upside potentiality and is loosely tied to intermediate term bond rates. The policyholder is taking no risk in variance of outcomes, but as a trade-off for that, the premiums are the highest because there are no risks. Similar in feel to a fixed mortgage in the housing industry.

This type of policy, which used to be very popular, is not so popular today because it lacks flexibility and because of the cost is so much higher due to the fact the insurance company takes all the risk and the client has no risk in the contract.

In between those two extremes is the territory where all the hybrids lay. There are arguably six different basic chassis that exist today and they run the gambit from universal life to variable universal life to indexed universal life and some sub-hybrids in between.

The majority of these are policies that allow for premiums to be adjusted year by year, and based on the premiums being adjusted, the cash value or the equity it builds allows the client to access for lifetime needs. This cash value or equity will grow slower or faster based upon how much money the premium payer is contributing to the contract.

The primary difference between these chassis is where the deposits will be invested once it is inside the cash value account of the contract.

In a universal life chassis, the money gets invested in a bond-like return account. It would feel most like a CD at the bank except it is not

FDIC insured. You are usually credited a slightly higher rate than five-year CDs being issued at that time, and it will also have a floor guarantee, usually of 1 or 2 percent, which would be the lowest rate it would earn during the lifetime of the contract. That rate is reset by the insurance company as interest rates go up or down through time.

The universal chassis used to be very popular, but as interest rates have been trending lower for many years now and remain low, other hybrids that have higher rate potential of return in the current market environment have taken over in the marketplace in popularity. The two permanent styles that seem to be most popular are variable universal life insurance and indexed universal life insurance.

Indexed universal life insurance takes the investment component of a policy and allows the consumer to either invest in a fixed component like a CD, with a guarantee, or in an index, either the stock market such as the S&P 500 or another index that might exist somewhere in the United States or elsewhere in the world. The client would get a return rate of that index over the period of time contractually listed, most commonly one year.

If the market index itself earns high returns during the crediting period, much like an adjustable mortgage, it will have a cap and a floor to the rate of return that gets applied during that period. As an example, if the ceiling cap was set at 10 percent, it means that if the market index being used earned 15 percent that year, the product would only credit up to the cap rate of 10 percent.

On the downside, there is also a floor guarantee, which is what many clients find appealing. This gives a policyholder the comfort that if the US stock market repeats a 2008-2009 condition and drops thirty or forty percent in one year, the policyholder, instead of getting that negative return to their cash investment, will get either a 0 or a 1 percent return applied to their portfolio so they can never lose money based upon market performance. This allows them to be invested in the market without having to worry about downside or loss. These policies are currently quite popular.

These types of contracts over time have shown to average 8.23 percent annualized return net of fees, with no taxes applied during the accumulation period. This figure is based on an S&P 500 Historical Return Calculator with a thirty-year look-back (https://dqydj.com/sp-500-return-calculator/). As an investment vehicle, this is very attractive to many consumers.

The second type of popular permanent chassis today is called variable universal life. This chassis takes the cash value and allows a client to actually select investments inside the policy from a menu that is provided to them by the insurance company. This menu frequently spans the risk continuum of the investment universe and many times exceeds fifty account choices that can be blended to simulate a professionally allocated investment portfolio.

This ability to mix and match a portfolio much like they might do in a traditional portfolio, with stocks, bonds, real estate, and cash in money market equivalent in any mix that fits their risk tolerance and time horizon, but in a very tax-favored manner makes it popular with sophisticated investors.

If these contracts are invested properly and in a growth-based asset allocation coupled with prudent fund selection, they have been shown the ability to earn higher than an indexed universal life policy. For example, a hypothetical historical performance of the Lincoln VULone (2014) can average 6.25 percent in annualized returns, net of fees with no tax over a long period of time, while still providing the life insurance protection the client needs for their family or business. Thus, they remain popular today (https://www.lfg.com/public/individual/exploreinsuranceannuities/lifeinsurance).

It is imperative to consider any surrender charges, fees, loan provisions, access to funds, riders offered, and/or any other items that may factor into a decision-making process regarding the product type.

How It Works: *(hypothetical example)*

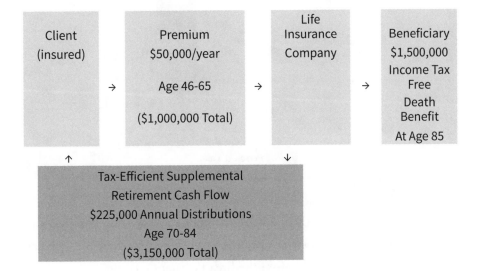

LIFE INSURANCE IN PERSONAL FINANCIAL PLANS

There are many ways life insurance is used in comprehensive financial plans. I will give a quick tour through many of the common ones over the next few pages, not in order of any priority. Let's start with where my initial story fit, and that is family income protection.

Where I first learned about life insurance in a financial plan, it was to provide a backstop against the loss of earnings from the bread earner or bread earners in a family.

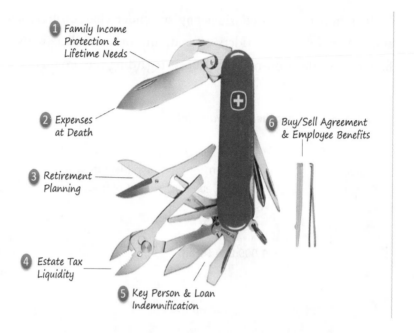

1. Family Income Protection & Lifetime Needs
2. Expenses at Death
3. Retirement Planning
4. Estate Tax Liquidity
5. Key Person & Loan Indemnification
6. Buy/Sell Agreement & Employee Benefits

You still find that a lot of insurance is put in force for families calculated to replace that lost paycheck for the family so their lifestyle can continue in the way it did before the bread earner's passing.

This is still the core use of coverage on the personal side. Creating tax-free dollars for families when they need them the most!

However, life insurance gets used in many, many other ways within a financial plan. Sometimes it is much more specific. For example, we see it used frequently just as a way of paying off loans and credit card debt. Many people want to have a policy to pay off their mortgages so their house is debt free; another way that we use the coverage is basically for final expenses.

Historically, another big reason why people bought insurance was to cover all their burial or final expenses for burial costs. That is still a common input today into the calculation for coverage for a family, so families do not have to liquidate something or search for money to pay for those final expenses that every family experiences.

Those are more traditional uses for insurance coverage on the family side, but due to the tax benefits of policies and the ability to grow cash inside of them very tax effectively, we see policies frequently getting used for families for lifetime income needs also. Specifically, college funding; one of the big benefits of using policies for college funding for children is that in in most cases, it does not show up on any of the forms used to apply for financial aid or financial benefits.

While the money is still there to help supplement or pay for school, it still allows a higher likelihood for a family to be able to facilitate getting loans, grants, or scholarships to partially pay for school costs, which are very high today.

Secondly, we see many clients use these as a way of building money for a specific need or goal in the future that is at least seven years or longer out in their timeframe. We see them used for down payment money to buy a vacation home for their family.

We see it used, most commonly, for retirement planning. Many clients do not or cannot, because of the rules the IRS gives us today, put enough money away in their 401(k) plans or their work-based plans to adequately reach their retirement goals in time, so they supplement that with other pots of money. The insurance policy can be a very tax-effective pot to grow a retirement supplement.

One other personal use that is very common for families today is, for larger estates, we use insurance for estate tax liquidity. Many families have a large estate tax that will be due in cash within nine months after a death. That tax can be into the millions of dollars in many cases. With a lack of liquidity planning, this tax due frequently forces families to sell some of their most valued assets and, in some cases, even heirloom properties or businesses to pay the tax.

In fact, that is exactly what happened to my family, which was one of the reasons that I found myself attracted to this business. I grew up on a family farm in northern California, and when my grandparents died they were unsophisticated in terms of financial planning. My family was left saddled with a large tax bill and bill for advisory fees due to their lack of appropriate documents to handle their estate distribution.

Long story short, our family was forced to sell our family farm to pay off the taxes and pay off the advisors. This forced us to move away from the farm and buy a house. Unfortunately for us, that land today is worth tens of millions of dollars because of where the farm happened to be, and somebody else is reaping the benefits of that. Plus, we lost the farm, which was a valuable source of income for our family.

That was a lesson I learned in arrears, and that is also why insurance is so valuable in an estate plan. If there is enough insurance to pay those taxes and advisor fees, a family never has to sell a business or sell a piece of real estate that is an heirloom property to pay the bill and settle the estate. That is a very, very important and common way that insurance gets used today. *(See the chart below as an example of the powerful leverage of life insurance for estate liquidity.)*

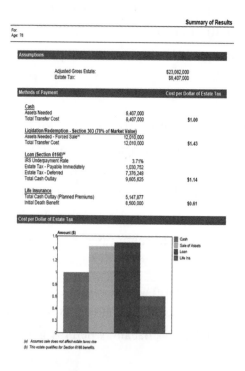

Lastly on the personal side, life insurance is frequently used for estate and charitable creation. The great leverage that life insurance provides allows for pennies on the dollar to be invested to create a tax-free legacy for family and charity alike.

LIFE INSURANCE IN BUSINESS PLANNING

On the business side, you see many uses for life insurance. One use is something called key person indemnity. Many businesses that we work with today have the owner and certain key people that bring measurable value to the business insured. If something were to happen to them unexpectedly, the business itself would suffer dollar losses in profit or sales.

What we do is put insurance in force on the lives of those owners or key employees, and the value of the insurance is adequate to be able to replenish the lost profit or sales to that business. Additionally, this allows that business time to find a replacement and train somebody up to adequately take that role over and put the business back in good financial standing.

We find that having that kind of coverage in place is also helpful for banks when they provide loans because they know that the company will not fall apart financially if somebody dies when the loan is still outstanding.

Another way that we use life insurance in the business scenario is for buy/sell agreement funding. If an uninsured owner dies unexpectedly, it is very hard for the surviving partners to find the discretionary after-tax cash flow, at a time they have lost their partner, to be able to run the business, pay expenses, and have enough money to pay off the estate of that deceased owner. So, insurance is used as a funding vehicle for the buyout of the deceased partner's interest.

For example, if you have two owners that are fifty-fifty partners and they have a two-million-dollar business, you would have a million dollars of insurance on each partner. That million dollars would be able to be transferred for the stock to the deceased person's estate tax free. There would be no harm to any cash flow or operations of the business. Each owner or estate walks away in a clean manner with no argument or control issues. That is a very common and important use of coverage today.

Another way that we use life insurance inside of a business is for loan indemnification. Many banks or other institutions require there is life insurance on the key people or owners to indemnify a loan, to make sure it would pay off in the event of a death.

We also see it used for pension funding. Many pensions will have insurance on key people inside the pension, which will allow the pension funding to be prefunded if a key person or an owner dies.

We also see insurance inside of a pension on individual employees because some employees would choose to have some of their retirement investments funding a policy, so if they die, their pension self-funds in advance, and then their spouse can get a pension check, even early, if that person dies before they have time to build that pension up themselves.

We also see it as a balance-sheet asset because healthy businesses have balance sheets that carry a lot of cash for either working capital use or rainy day money against a tough environment in their economy. Today that cash in the current environment is not earning very much interest (less than 1 percent), and what it does earn gets taxed as ordinary income rates.

So, if you park that same cash inside of a life insurance policy, that cash return inside of the policy is tax protected and causes no tax and in many cases has the potential to earn a higher return on investment than the balance-sheet cash was at their bank, while still providing the death benefit for the other purposes that I mentioned earlier. That is a very effective use, as well. The policy in this case does double duty, providing answers to two goals in one vehicle!

_____

We also see it used as an executive or a key person fringe benefit. Many companies will give additional supplemental life insurance coverage, provided to an executive or key employee, paid for by the company for that executive or owner, as a fringe benefit.

That is framed as either executive supplemental life insurance or in some cases it is put together with a certain kind of policy to provide supplemental retirement income, which we call either non-qualified deferred compensation or a supplemental executive retirement program. This is very common across the US today.

LIFE INSURANCE AND TAXATION

Life insurance has always been powerful because of the tax advantages and the unique benefits that it provides. First and foremost, the death benefit itself, correctly accounted for, is paid to the beneficiary of the policy 100 percent income tax free! Every dollar of death benefit is available for the use in which it is intended. Which is a benefit compared to most other investments, where you would have to pay some amount of tax to access cash.

The second component of it that is so valuable is the tax-free inside build-up of the cash or equity investment during the accumulation phase. As it grows and compounds, there is no 1099 or K1 statement that must be applied on a person's or a business's annual tax return. This allows the compounding equity to grow faster than other comparative investments. This absence of tax drag can be very impactful on a policyholder's net return.

Another underappreciated benefit a policyholder has in these chassis is they are able to re-allocate their investments around within the policy tax free. There is no capital gain tax levied as they move money within the policy amongst different investment sub-accounts. This increases the chance of a better long-term return, as a policyholder and his advisor are not hampered by tax drag when an asset re-allocation is called for due to market conditions or goal changes.

Policies can also be exchanged via a section 1035 tax-free exchange to a completely different policy, as well, providing the client a lot of flexibility should their goals or situation change. This is frequently enacted to purchase a policy with improved features. Like any strategy, this is not done without risks that need to be carefully considered by working with a professional. Two major risks are one's ability to qualify for a new product based upon health and starting a new two-year contestability period that provides the insurance carrier the right to challenge any claims during that timeframe.

The client also has access to investment equity, including the profits under what is called FIFO (first-in, first-out) treatment instead of LIFO (last-in, first-out) treatment, which is accounting terminology. What it means practically is that on most of the policies available in the marketplace, the policyholder can access the profits tax free via a net zero-percent interest loan.

This is a completely unique tax benefit that no other investment vehicle has at its disposal! Caution is warranted both in the design and ongoing funding of these chassis to avoid overfunding the contract, thus converting it into a modified endowment contract (MEC). This would convert the tax status on cash values to annuity-like treatment, which is far less favorable. Always be aware of the seven pay funding number that will be listed on your policy proposal for awareness of this limit!!

In essence, whether it is a living need or a death benefit need, if handled properly a life insurance policy is one of a kind in the sense that it can be used in lifetime and death and not have any income taxes levied at any point in the complete life cycle of the product. This makes life insurance completely unique in the financial universe.

There are certain policy designs, unique features, and riders that if you put maximum non-MEC contributions in the policies, as the tax laws have allowed since 1986, the "7702 corridor" is hit. What the corridor relates to is, for tax purposes today, there must always be a certain "corridor" of extra death benefit over and beyond the cash value that builds inside of the policy.

We can purposely design a policy where as the cash value grows, the death benefit goes up. The big advantage here is the policyholder receives increased death benefit through time but does not have to requalify health through another physical, and their death benefit grows. Continually I see this strategy being used to further leverage premiums being paid. The longer the insured lives without withdrawing cash value, the policy will continue to increase death benefit beyond the original base level.

RIDERS AND ADD-ON OPTIONS

There are many riders, or add-ons, that you can optionally attach to life insurance policies today. Some of the more popular ones cover long-term care indemnification. All our clients in financial planning have a potential risk against either spouse becoming sick or hurt and needing to pay for convalescent care or home care.

The problem today is that Medicare does not cover that exposure adequately, so a family could deplete their retirement nest egg very quickly having to pay that kind of expense. Insurance companies have developed riders that you can add on to your life insurance policy that will provide protection against the cost of the long-term care exposure and will, in addition to providing life insurance, also provide a pot of money to pay the cost for the family so it does not eat into their retirement plan.

Another type of rider that is very popular is the additional death benefit option. This allows you to purchase more coverage periodically through time without having to go through another physical or medical examination if your needs change and you have a need for more coverage in the future.

Another rider that is very common is called a waiver of premium. The waiver of premium rider provides if the policyholder gets sick or hurt during the lifetime of the contract. The premiums are then waived until the policyholder is well enough that they can go back to work and pay for their premiums again so the policy is not lost. There are constantly new riders being developed in the industry to help make the policies much more comprehensive in their use.

There is so much information today with the Internet Age on insurance that the most important thing, we feel, is to try and have a logical process that allows you to filter out the noise and the non-relevant material in shopping for coverage.

What we highly recommend is that you find a licensed and qualified agent to assist you in the shopping. Whether they are assisting you or you are doing it yourself, there are some fundamental steps that we think are important to tilt the odds toward you getting both a good value policy as well as an insurance company that is going to be stable and safe.

One of the things that we highly recommend people do is a search of the rating services for a particular insurance company in terms of their ratings to pay claims. There are many rating services, each with their own methodology. *(See chart below for a sample company ratings report.)*

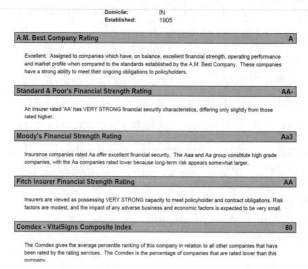

| Domicile: | IN |
| Established: | 1905 |

A.M. Best Company Rating — **A**

Excellent. Assigned to companies which have, on balance, excellent financial strength, operating performance and market profile when compared to the standards established by the A.M. Best Company. These companies have a strong ability to meet their ongoing obligations to policyholders.

Standard & Poor's Financial Strength Rating — **AA-**

An insurer rated 'AA' has VERY STRONG financial security characteristics, differing only slightly from those rated higher.

Moody's Financial Strength Rating — **Aa3**

Insurance companies rated Aa offer excellent financial security. The Aaa and Aa group constitute high grade companies, with the Aa companies rated lower because long-term risk appears somewhat larger.

Fitch Insurer Financial Strength Rating — **AA**

Insurers are viewed as possessing VERY STRONG capacity to meet policyholder and contract obligations. Risk factors are modest, and the impact of any adverse business and economic factors is expected to be very small.

Comdex - VitalSigns Composite Index — **80**

The Comdex gives the average percentile ranking of this company in relation to all other companies that have been rated by the rating services. The Comdex is the percentage of companies that are rated lower than this company.

	A.M. Best	Standard & Poor's	Moody's	Fitch	Weiss
1.	A++ Superior	AAA Extemely Strong	Aaa Exceptional	AAA Exceptionally Strong	A+ Excellent
2.	A+ Superior	AA+ Very Strong	Aa1 Excellent	AA+ Very Strong	A Excellent
3.	A Excellent	AA Very Strong	Aa2 Excellent	AA Very Strong	A- Excellent
4.	A- Excellent	AA- Very Strong	Aa3 Excellent	AA- Very Strong	B+ Good
5.	B++ Very Good	A+ Strong	A1 Good	A+ Strong	B Good
6.	B+ Good	A Strong	A2 Good	A Strong	B- Good
7.	B Fair	A- Strong	A3 Good	A- Strong	C+ Fair
8.	B- Fair	BBB+ Good	Baa1 Adequate	BBB+ Good	C Fair
9.	C++ Marginal	BBB Good	Baa2 Adequate	BBB Good	C- Fair
10.	C+ Marginal	BBB- Good	Baa3 Adequate	BBB- Good	D+ Weak
11.	C Weak	BB+ Marginal	Ba1 Questionable	BB+ Moderately Weak	D Weak
12.	C- Weak	BB Marginal	Ba2 Questionable	BB Moderately Weak	D- Weak
13.	D Poor	BB- Marginal	Ba3 Questionable	BB- Moderately Weak	E+ Very Weak
14.	E Under State Supervision	B+ Weak	B1 Poor	B+ Weak	E Very Weak
15.	F In Liquidation	B Weak	B2 Poor	B Weak	E- Very Weak
16.		B- Weak	B3 Poor	B- Weak	F Failed
17.		CCC+ Very Weak	Caa1 Very Poor	CCC+ Very Weak	
18.		CCC Very Weak	Caa2 Very Poor	CCC Very Weak	
19.		CCC- Very Weak	Caa3 Very Poor	CCC- Very Weak	
20.		CC Extremely Weak	Ca Extremely Poor	CC Very Weak	
21.			C Lowest	C Very Weak	
22.				DDD Insolvent	
23.				DD Insolvent	
24.				D Insolvent	

What we highly recommend is that somebody stick to the companies that have at least the higher tiers of ratings across all the rating services, and if you follow the shopping process similar to the one that I show in the chart below, it will help a client progress gradually through a series of steps to be able to ultimately get down to the point where they have one or two companies that have the best pricing and great rating service reviews.

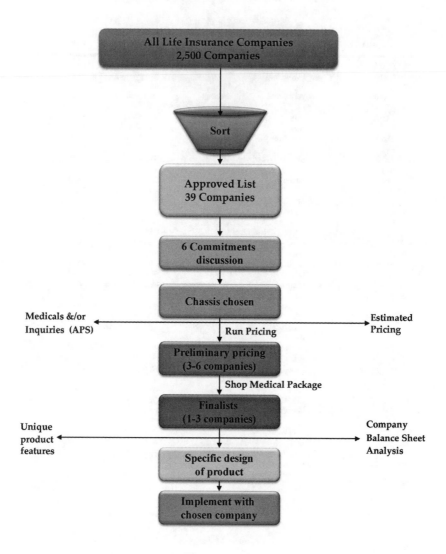

Once the prospective policyholder has completed their underwriting process, and companies respond with favorable ratings, the combination of those three criteria provides assurances the policyholder will receive good value.

Miscellaneous Thoughts: As life happens, sometimes coverages that were in place for personal or business purposes are no longer needed.

In response to this came in the arrival of a secondary market for life insurance. What many people are not aware of is that they can take a policy that they no longer need, and it can be sold to institutional investors. These institutions buy policies from the initial owner and pay the premium themselves for the rest of the lifetime of that coverage and then collect the death benefit. Their goal is to make a profit.

In return, the benefit to the policyholder is they will receive a check today in return for selling that policy to the institutional investor. The former policyowner has no further rights to the policy and no further premiums to pay. And they have a check in their hands.

These options should be explored before they just lapse or give up a policy completely for little or no surrender value.

Life insurance is the only product that is always there when you need it the most. I have never seen a family, an investor, a fiduciary, or a trustee that thought an estate, a business, or family had too much liquidity at the time of receiving a death claim check. It is the only product that can be a great benefit to a financial or business plan for the long term, but is always there from the first day on, when you need it the most.

Professional Profile:

Derek B. Ferriera, CFP®, CLU©, CFC©, REBC©, CBEC©

Derek.Ferriera@LFG.com | 408-879-4211 |

www.MYcsolutions.com

With over thirty years of experience, Derek B. Ferriera brings a customized comprehensive approach to help translate his clients' financial goals into action steps. His experience on over a thousand cases provides clients the benefit of knowing that their plan will run through rigorous design testing and convey sophisticated solutions, while Derek acts as a motivating catalyst until completion.

Derek is an active member of the financial planning community and keeps abreast the changes and innovations in the industry. He is a regular presenter at National Training Conferences for Lincoln Financial Advisors and Sagemark Consulting, as well as a certified CPE instructor, providing continuing education for local CPAs.

As a graduate of Cal Poly State University, San Luis Obispo, Derek began his career in 1984 at John Hancock until his transition to Sagemark Consulting as Founder and Managing Partner of C Solutions. Derek grew up in the Bay Area and enjoys sports, music, CrossFit, and travel. Derek lives in Morgan Hill, has two children, Alex and Andrea, and is accompanied by two dogs and two cats.

CHAPTER ELEVEN

CHARITABLE PLANNING STRATEGIES

By J. Todd Anderson

THE WORLD NEEDS DOERS AND DONORS

Giving back, paying it forward, making a difference, providing a helping hand, and serving others. There are many different ways to describe charitable interests and there are many motivations for being both a "doer" and a "donor." It is likely that you have had some experience doing both.

"Doing" gifts of time, energy, expertise, and service are how many of us learned to be charitable. For me, personally, that was through the example of family members and the Boy Scouts of America. The oath of the Boy Scouts says to "help other people at all times," and their slogan is, "Do a good turn daily." Doing a good turn daily and finding ways to help other people and our community were second nature as I progressed to be an Eagle Scout. Whether it was helping a family clean up their yard, shoveling the snow for an elderly neighbor, or carving hiking trails in the mountains, I was learning how to be "doer."

Our experience in being a "donor" may have also started small for many of us. I remember saving my own dimes and then going door to door to ask my neighbors to add their dimes to the March of Dimes, which had a mission to improve the health of mothers and babies.

Most of us have some experience like this, well before we were concerned about the financial, tax, and estate-planning implications and applications for donating to charities. Being a doer and a donor growing up shaped my interest in continuing to do this as an adult and made me passionate about helping advise countless clients about charitable planning during my more than thirty-two years as a Financial Advisor.

While we could focus this entire chapter on encouraging readers to be a doer and donor, we will assume all readers have some level of motivation to give back and help others. And, we will assume you might be interested in "give smart strategies," which will also reduce your income and/or estate taxes in the process. Thus, we will explore ways to take your charitable planning to the next level in the context of a holistic financial planning process, through "give smart strategies."

ARE WE OKAY? IS OUR COMMUNITY OKAY?

Over thirty-two years as a financial advisor has taught me that whether clients have $300,000 in net worth or $30 million in net worth, all have similar fears about running out of money. Clients have more motivation and more capacity to give back if we can address and answer the question, "Are we okay?"

Our experience shows that clients who engage in a holistic financial planning process become more involved in charitable planning. This process includes sophisticated, Monte Carlo simulation modeling, and "what-if" scenario development, which can help answer the question, "Are we okay?" through "stress testing" their financial world.

Below, you will see the Family Legacy Pyramid that I like to use as we discuss this process with clients and work through the progression of planning, where the focus moves from building security and confidence for the clients and their family and then works toward the ability to dedicate resources to charitable planning.

FAMILY LEGACY PYRAMID

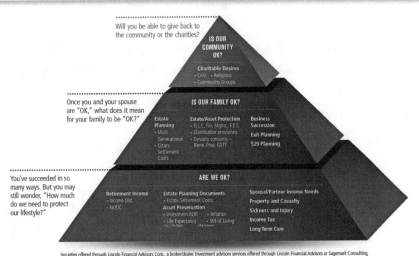

Will you be able to give back to the community or the charities?

IS OUR COMMUNITY OK?

Charitable Desires
• Civic • Religious
• Community Groups

Once you and your spouse are "OK," what does it mean for your family to be "OK?"

IS OUR FAMILY OK?

Estate Planning	Estate/Asset Protection	Business
• Multi Generational	• D,L,C, Fin. Mgmt., F.E.T.	Succession
• Estate Settlement Costs	• Distribution provisions	Exit Planning
	• Dynasty concerns — Bene. Prep, GSTT	529 Planning

You've succeeded in so many ways. But you may still wonder, "How much do we need to protect our lifestyle?"

ARE WE OK?

Retirement Income	Estate Planning Documents	Spousal/Partner Income Needs
• Income Dist.	• Estate Settlement Costs	Property and Casualty
• NQDC	**Asset Preservation**	Sickness and Injury
	• Investment ROR • Inflation	Income Tax
	• Life Expectancy • Std of Living	Long Term Care
	• D,L,C, Fin. Mgmt. • Rd. Tolerance	

Securities offered through Lincoln Financial Advisors Corp., a broker/dealer. Investment advisory services offered through Lincoln Financial Advisors or Sagemark Consulting, a division of Lincoln Financial Advisors, a registered investment advisor. Insurance offered through Lincoln affiliates and other fine companies. CRN-1748079-033017
Lincoln Financial Advisors Corp. and its representatives do not provide legal or tax advice.

After first working with clients to build a retirement income financial model, we then stress test their situation. For example, we look forward without the benefit of a crystal ball and model what would to their financial world if we had higher inflation, or poor investment returns, or if income tax rates go up, or we live to be 105 years old! All concerns that could potentially cause their money to run out before "blast off." When we work through these scenarios with a client and are able to demonstrate a high probability of never running out of money, even with stressing their situation, it helps them understand that they are "okay," and it allows them to start to focus more resources in helping others, where they can ask, "Is my community okay?"

One couple we work with, Bill and Jane, had a $20 million net worth and were in their late fifties as we started this process. They had not done any substantial charitable giving and did not foresee an ability to do it in the future. Through a holistic financial planning process, and stress testing "what-if scenarios," they were able to feel for the first time that they were "okay."

This allowed them to move forward in developing a plan to help several charitable organizations that were important to them by incorporating "give smart strategies." In their case, they had a highly appreciated asset that they donated to a charitable remainder trust and enjoyed substantial tax savings and an income for their lifetimes, with the remainder interest going to the charity. But none of that would have happened without the modeling and having confidence that they were "okay." We will talk more about Charitable Trusts later in this chapter.

Without question, when clients know that they are "okay," it allows them to then focus on, "Is my community okay?" and it allows us to serve them in an area we are passionate about, which is charitable planning. The rest of this chapter will focus on some of my favorite "give smart strategies" for charitable planning.

GIVE SMART!

This subject could fill a book rather than a chapter, so I will focus on "give smart ideas" that can be high impact and that many of our clients find useful.

GIVE WHAT?

Most people think of contributing cash to charity first, where in many cases it should be the last resort. Examples of assets that may make sense to give rather than cash include:

- Appreciated Stock or Mutual Funds
- Appreciated Real Estate
- Privately held business interests

- IRAs

Most of these assets allow some level of tax leverage, because if you sold them without first donating them to a charity, you would pay capital gains tax and, in some cases, ordinary income tax. However, a charity can receive appreciated assets and liquidate them with no income taxes due, while you realize some level of tax deduction, depending on the strategy you are using.

I can think of an example where clients had made a commitment to always pay 10 percent of their income or gain as an annual tithe to their church. In the past they had always made those donations by writing a check. As we worked together on their holistic financial plan and stress tested their world to make sure they were okay, we found that they had significant appreciated stock that was available to make charitable donations rather than cash.

In this case they also had a very concentrated position in a stock that they also wanted to lighten up on but had hesitated to do because of the capital gains taxes selling it would trigger. Many charities have a very simple process to transfer shares of stock or mutual funds "in kind" (i.e., the position isn't sold; the positions are just moved to the charity).

Then, once the charity receives it, that asset can be sold and diversified, if desired, or even held long term, depending on the form of account that is established when the donation is made and whether it is an outright gift or some type of deferred gift, which we will talk about soon. And the client enjoyed the same tax deduction as if they had written a check!

GIVING IRA ASSETS?

Another great and fairly new "give smart strategy" is a process for gifting of IRA assets. In January of 2016 Congress passed the Consolidated Appropriations Act of 2016 to make permanent the rules allowing Qualified Charitable Distributions (QCDS) for individual retirement accounts (IRAs). Or, at least "permanent until they change it again," which Congress has a tendency to do! But for now, it's a super cool "give smart strategy" where it fits.

To qualify for the strategy you must be seventy and a half or older and the transfer must go directly to the charity, and it is limited to $100,000 per year. Many Americans have a significant portion of their investment assets in quailed retirement accounts like IRAs, so having an avenue to use some of these resources for charitable giving can make a significant difference in their capacity to give.

Also, for many people it can help with the problem of having to take taxable required minimum distributions (RMD's) that they don't really need for living expenses but are forced to pay taxes on. Our client, Margie, is seventy-one and she is being forced to take RMDs from her IRA annually to avoid the 50 percent penalty tax that could be levied if she failed to take the distribution. Margie's IRA is currently valued at $500,000, so she is required to take a minimum distribution of $19,000 this year.

She doesn't need the distribution for living expenses, as she has a nice pension, Social Security, and other investments that provide income. And, she is concerned that taking the RMDs could affect her income tax situation and put her in a higher bracket. We found that Margie had experienced the loss of loved ones to cancer and that she was very fond of a cancer research foundation and would like to support it financially.

Margie instructed us to transfer $19,000 from her IRA account directly to the charitable foundation that focuses on cancer research. She was able to satisfy her annual RMD, make a contribution of $19,000 to her favorite charity, and pay no income tax on retirement assets that had deferred gains for many, many years. The only loser in the process was the IRS, but Margie was fine with that, as the IRS isn't her charity of choice!

In making a Qualified Charitable Distribution, Margie doesn't receive a tax deduction, but when doing the math we find that it is better to avoid the tax on the RMD than it is to take a tax deduction if she used non-IRA assets to give to the charity.

GIVING SMART AFTER "BLAST OFF"?

Up to this point we have been talking about outright giving of cash or appreciated assets or IRAs to charities for their use. However, several of the strategies that we widely utilize with clients defer the gift and use of assets by the charity until sometime later, or even after you "blast off." You heard that term earlier in this chapter. I have never been fond of the terms "passing away," "expiring," or "dying." I prefer "blasting off," which seems a little more exciting and easier to discuss with clients.

I have personally incorporated a "blast off give smart strategy" with one of my favorite charities, my alma mater, to complete and/or expand a student leadership endowment I helped establish. I make annual contributions to fund the endowment, while part of my annual contribution is used for ongoing programs at the university. When I make my contribution, I also qualify for a matching gift from our company to expand the gift. Even then, I would like to do something bigger than I am able to do at this stage of my life, and I want to make sure that if I "blast off" before I've completed funding the endowment that it will still be accomplished or even expanded beyond what my original goals were.

For me, a very simple solution was naming the university as a beneficiary of one of my life insurance contracts. In this case, just a partial beneficiary, as the university is the beneficiary of 20 percent of the death benefit and my family is the beneficiary of the other 80 percent. Hopefully I will have a long life, and as my family grows older and has less need for the life insurance death benefit, I will likely increase the percentage that goes to my university.

This planning makes sure that if I "blast off" prematurely, or if I have a long life, my charitable giving goals for my university will have been met, or exceeded. Consider the leverage of life insurance to expand charitable giving beyond what you might be able to do during your lifetime. It's a great "give smart strategy".

SEPARATING SMART TAX PLANNING FROM YOUR DECISIONS TO DONATE TO CHARITY—THE MAGIC OF THE DONOR-ADVISED FUND:

Next I want to explore two of my favorite strategies that can provide substantial tax savings now, even though the charities may not benefit immediately.

Many people call the Donor-Advised Fund (DAF) "the new Family Foundation." Family Foundations have been around for decades, but Donor-Advised Funds are fairly new and, increasingly, we see clients use a DAF instead of a Foundation and there are a number of reasons for that.

First, it's likely that a DAF will be less complicated to set up and will be easier and more cost-effective to administer into the future. Many clients also do not want to be forced to make annual distributions from a Foundation until they are prepared to do that. With a Family Foundation, 5 percent of the assets must be distributed annually. With the Donor-Advised Fund there is no such requirement.

There are some other advantages for Donor-Advised Funds. For example, if you are donating closely held stock or real estate, with a DAF you can deduct the fair market value at the time you contributed; with a private foundation you can only deduct your cost basis.

It also has a higher capacity to give as a percentage of your adjusted gross income (AGI), where with a DAF you can contribute 60 percent for cash or 30 percent for appreciated assets, where a Foundation is 50 percent for cash and 20 percent for appreciated assets.

However, the thing our clients like the best about a Donor-Advised Fund, and that I love as their Financial Advisor, is their ability to use their

DAF as a tax-planning tool and separate their desire to fund a specific charity from smart and timely tax planning.

Let me explain: Often, in the fourth quarter of the year, our clients who have Donor-Advised Funds are looking with us at their capacity to give and their current tax situation and deciding whether they want to reduce their current taxable income by donating more to the Donor-Advised Fund now, which they will, at some point down the road, donate to qualified charity of their choice. This process allows us to increase contributions during high income years or when big bonuses have been paid or during the year they sell their business or have some other activity that created higher-than-normal taxable income. While a direct contribution to a qualified charity should be considered as well, a Donor-Advised Fund captures the upfront tax deduction now and allows for a deferred or controlled distribution to charity rather than all at once.

Under the Tax Cuts and Jobs Act of 2017 the concept of "bunching deductions," to allow you to itemize in some years and in others to take the $24,000 standard deduction, makes a DAF strategy even more compelling and flexible. Because the SALT deduction (State and Local Taxes) is now capped at $10,000 we find many clients will not itemize unless they have a big charitable contribution year and/or mortgage interest expense. So bunching charitable deductions during certain years will make sense, and a DAF helps with that.

When they make a contribution to their DAF, they receive an immediate charitable tax deduction. As we discussed earlier, this is even more powerful when that donation is made with appreciated assets rather than cash. But, writing a check works just fine also.

Ultimately, when we decide to make a payout from the Donor-Advised Fund to the charity of our choice, it does need to be a 501c3 charity. But, it doesn't even need to happen during the donor's lifetime, as you could have family members or others named as successors to continue to make gifts from your DAF even after you have "blasted off."

CAN FAMILY FOUNDATIONS STILL "GIVE SMART STRATEGIES"?

There are areas where Foundations have advantages over a DAF. For example, when a client wants a high level of control and involvement and they would like to make donations to non- 501c3 charities. Maybe they are trying to give money directly to an individual or family in need or get involved at a level not permitted in a DAF. Or, for example, where they would like to have family members charged with running the day-to-day activities of the Foundation and, subject to certain limitations, provide some salary or employment benefits. In this case, a Family Foundation may be the best charitable entity for them to use.

While I am a big fan of and personally use a Donor-Advised Fund in my charitable planning, Family Foundations are still a very important part of philanthropy in our country, and each family should consider with their advisors which "give smart strategy" would be right for their planning. Either can provide a very valuable tax-planning tool while laying a foundation for a lifetime of gifting and beyond.

A DONOR-ADVISED FUND "GIVE SMART STORY."

Our client, George, and his wife, Margaret, are founders of a technology company that has experienced rapid growth and that he was positioning to sell and eventually retire. They had almost no basis in the company, but their stock was now worth over $40 million. One of George and Margaret's financial and charitable planning goals was to always to donate 10 percent of their income or assets to charity. They also wanted to establish a fund that would support future charitable giving that would keep them involved in doing good after they sold their company.

Through the planning process, George and Margaret decided to transfer $4 million of privately held stock in their company to a Donor-Advised Fund we helped them establish. Being in a 37 percent combined tax bracket for capitals gains and with almost zero basis in the stock, they will save almost $1.5 million in capital gains taxes after the business is sold, and he received a $4 million itemized deduction for their charitable contribution to the DAF in the year the stock was contributed.

Being in a 56 percent combined Federal and State marginal tax bracket, George and Margaret saved over $2.2 million in income taxes with the deduction. *And* their Donor-Advised Fund is still holding $4 million in stock, which will hopefully appreciate more and turn to cash soon as they sell the company. That asset is also outside of their taxable estate, so if something unexpected happened to George and Margaret, and Uncle Sam came calling, there would be no estate taxes due on this $4 million in stock or cash.

There are phase-outs and other limitations that could limit the ability to fully deduct the contribution, and this is one of many reasons it's critical that we coordinate with a client's CPA and their estate attorney.

THE MAGIC OF A CHARITABLE REMAINDER TRUST (CRT)

Since 1969 countless families have used Charitable Remainder Trusts to increase their incomes while reducing their income and estate taxes and benefiting charities. What does a CRT do? First, a CRT is another tax-planning tool that would, for example, let you convert a highly appreciated asset like stock or real estate into a lifetime income. Yes, you can use cash, but that usually should be the last resort if we have appreciated assets to use.

Establishing and funding a CRT now reduces your income taxes now and estate taxes when you die. You pay no capital gains taxes when the asset is sold, and it lets you help one or more charities down the road that have special meaning to you.

For example, we were working with clients John and Mary who knew they were "okay" and wanted to help their community now. The best way for them to do that was through a donation of highly appreciated, non-income-producing property. They had owned undeveloped land that provided no income and required annual property tax payments. They had a very low basis in the land, and they had no future use for the property. They had thought about selling it and then taking the net amount and investing it to support their retirement income or donate to charity, but they had always backed away because of the large capital gains taxes that would be due.

John and Mary decided to donate the appreciated land to a Charitable Remainder Trust that they established. Once inside the trust, the land was sold to a buyer, and that provided $1,000,000 of cash into the Charitable Remainder Trust.

That could then be invested in a diversified strategy, and John and Sally elected to have a 5 percent lifetime income stream payed to them, which would continue until both of them had "blasted off." At that time, whatever remained (that is where the "remainder" word in Charitable Remainder Trust comes from) would go to the charity of their choice.

In this type of an arrangement there is not a full tax deduction for the charitable contribution because a lifetime income stream is retained, but there can still be a significant tax deduction depending on the age of the donors and whether there are one or two people enjoying a lifetime income interest.

But, that partial tax deduction combined with avoiding all of the capital gains taxes can be significant. And now John and Mary could enjoy income from the full $1 million rather than what would have been a much lower "after tax" number if they had sold the property outside of the CRT.

For clients who also could be subject to estate taxes down the road, moving this asset to a Donor-Advised Fund, or in this case to a Charitable Trust, does move it outside of the taxable estate. Eventually after the second person has passed away, in the case of a married couple, there would be no estate tax due on the asset.

There are many other variations of Charitable Trusts. The one I have just described would be a Charitable Remainder Uni-Trust (CRUT). When considering strategies with Advisors you may find that other forms of Charitable Trust have application. This would include Charitable Annuity Trusts, Charitable Lead Trusts, Net Income Trusts, and many other variations. They can be very effective planning tools for you and for the charity, although you will want to avoid them if the IRS is one of your favorite charities! Not!

One great "give smart strategy" twist combines a Charitable Remainder Trust and A Donor-Advised Fund. In this design, rather than naming a specific charity to receive the remainder interest, they establish a Donor-Advised Fund and name it as the beneficiary. When they pass away, it allows successor trustees for the Donor-Advised Fund, in this case maybe their children, to continue to do charitable good over time.

There are so many creative things that can be done with charitable trusts when it fits a client's goals and capacity to give.

A ZERO ESTATE TAX PLAN AND GIVE SMART STRATEGY WHERE THE IRS LOSES AND CHARITY WINS:

Depending on the size of their taxable estates, many Americans do not fully understand that the IRS could be a major beneficiary of their lifetime of work when they "blast off." Our current estate tax law dictates that if an individual "blasts off" with more than $11,180,000 in assets, or married couples have more than $22,360,000 in assets (these are the 2018 rules), they will face an estate tax of 40 percent on assets over those limits.

Our clients with assets over these limits really have three potential beneficiaries of their assets. The assets can go to family, it can go to charity, or it can go to the IRS, or a combination of the three. We ask clients to assign a percentage to how much they would like to go where. Oftentimes they will put something like family 80 percent, charity 20 percent; I have yet to have anybody give any percentage to the IRS; it is usually a big, fat zero!

However, in many cases their estate plan and financial plan is not geared to make that happen. But an individual or a family can take the IRS out of the beneficiary lineup if they designate that their estate assets over their exemption limit (i.e., the $22.4 million for a married couple) go to charity at their "blast off" or incorporate other charitable strategies that will allow them to reach this goal.

This strategy came into play for clients who desire to leave assets to his children but not at a level that would make them lazy or not wanting to succeed on their own. Thus, they felt leaving assets up to the exemption limit more than satisfied what they would like to go to family and allowed them to get creative with us in their planning to make sure everything above those limits went to charity.

They actually became very motivated to continue to grow their net worth and wealth when they felt like they were now actually working for charities they cared about. This helped them develop a great passion for charitable giving and a renewed purpose for their future.

As part of a zero state tax plan a very important strategy is to consider what assets do not receive a step up in basis. Those would include IRA accounts and tax-deferred annuities. Often we name a charity as the beneficiary for those accounts, as the rules allow the charity to receive that asset without any tax and for you to avoid any income and/or estate tax in that process.

YOUR CHARITABLE PLAN—MOVING FORWARD AND GIVING BACK

I am very passionate about holistic financial planning being the key driver to help create clarity and confidence in charitable giving. And, that starting with the process of confirming that, "We are okay," allows us to focus more resources on making sure, "Our community is okay."

As a family, developing a family mission statement related to charitable planning, potentially giving children a "giving allowance," having a family volunteer day, and deciding as a family what charities to contribute to can all help develop both doers and donors as a legacy to our lifetime of work.

Remember the lessons that we have learned in this chapter as you work with your Financial Advisors to integrate charitable planning into your financial and estate planning. Coordination is critical, and when your Financial Advisor is working with your estate planning attorney and your CPA in a coordinated way, great things can happen.

So, remember the world needs both doers and donors. Work with your Advisors to find out if you are "okay" or are on the path to be "okay" so you can focus more of your wealth to making your community "okay." Learn some of these give smart strategies that might have application for your situation, like the Donor-Advised Fund, Charitable Trust, or many other avenues that are available.

And, if you have a large estate, consider taking the IRS out of the equation so they are no longer one of your beneficiaries, and decide what you want to go to family and to charity instead.

I have just touched a limited number of "give smart strategies" in this chapter, but I hope it will inspire a few of you to take a thoughtful and coordinated approach when considering the integration or expansion of charitable planning in your financial future.

Professional Profile:

J. Todd Anderson, CFP

JTodd.Anderson@LFG.com | 801-930-6478 |

www.sagemarkslc.com

J. Todd Anderson has earned the CERTIFIED FINANCIAL PLAN-NER™ Professional certification (CFP°) and is a member of Sagemark Consulting Private Wealth Services. Todd started his career after earning a Business Finance degree from Weber State University. He has over thir-ty-two years of experience in holistic/comprehensive wealth planning dis-ciplines and lives by the creed of «Serve First, Serve Last, Serve Always.»

Todd credits his affiliation with a client-centered company and work-ing with great Team Members and Partners as the reason he has enjoyed a successful career serving his clients. Todd is all about "life balance" and spreads a message of GOAL: "Get Outside and Live" with everyone.

Thus, if Todd's not in the office you are likely to find him skiing, hiking, mountain biking, golfing, fly fishing, hunting, or on some other crazy adventure with family, friends, clients, or anyone he can drag along. Todd and his wife, Jill, have one son, Jay T, who recently graduated from the University of Utah with an Honors Business Finance degree and is now working for Microsoft as a Financial Analyst.

Brought to you by a group of highly successful financial experts, *Master Your Financial Success* brings you insights into the most significant areas of your Financial Life. Use this book to guide you through your toughest, yet most fulfilling retirement, family, and legacy decisions.

You'll immediately benefit by learning from others' real life experiences on:

- Income Distribution and Strategies for Retirement
- Sheltering Income and Assets from Unnecessary Taxes
- Preserving Family Stewardship and Family Wealth

- Understanding the Economics of Life Insurance
- Planning Considerations Specific to Business Owners and Executives
- Developing an Impactful Charitable Giving Strategy

The council in this book comes from the collective wisdom and time-tested advice employed by the eleven authors who represent some of the brightest minds in the Financial Planning community. They collaborate by using best practices and the most effective and current planning techniques for the ultimate benefit of each unique client. They choose to work and live by a shared philosophy of "Serve First, Serve Last, and Serve Always."

ENDORSEMENTS

WILL FULLER, PRESIDENT, ANNUITY SOLUTIONS, LINCOLN FINANCIAL DISTRIBUTORS, LINCOLN FINANCIAL NETWORK

In a time when few Americans have pensions and Social Security is unlikely to provide enough to live comfortably in retirement, there is more pressure than ever on individual savings. The authors reflect the philosophy behind Lincoln's independent financial advisor network and share our commitment to holistic financial planning and helping Americans have sufficient savings and protected income that lasts through retirement.

DAVID BERKOWITZ, PRESIDENT, LINCOLN FINANCIAL NETWORK

Serve first, last, and always is our creed at Lincoln Financial Network and guides our client-first philosophy that underlies everything we do. This group of advisors truly embraces those values by offering their collective expertise to help address critical issues that impact retirement and financial planning.

JOHN DIMONDA, SENIOR VICE PRESIDENT, LINCOLN FINANCIAL ADVISORS

The authors have built their practices providing financial planning support for clients across age groups, generations, income levels, and unique family situations. They bring real-life experience and invaluable thought leadership for the collective benefit of all those who hope for a more secure financial future.

CARRIE CHELKO, SENIOR VICE PRESIDENT & CHIEF COUNSEL, LINCOLN FINANCIAL GROUP DISTRIBUTION

In today's market environment with ever-increasing challenges and regulatory changes, it's more important than ever for people to work with experienced financial advisors and planners to help them achieve their goals. It's wonderful to see this group of advisors share their resources and lessons learned along the way with all those contemplating their own financial futures and retirement needs.

PETER GIACCIO, CHIEF EXECUTIVE OFFICER, THE RESOURCE GROUP

These fourteen advisors each have a story of their own—having built successful practices and developed significant experience on a wide range of financial planning strategies. However, they've come together for the greater good to share their real-life experiences and help to influence the financial well-being of people from all walks of life as they plan for their financial futures.